The Dream of Deliverance in American Politics
(1986)

Women of Academe
(coauthored with Nadya Aisenberg)
(1988)

Women Lawyers—Rewriting the Rules
(1994)

CARE AND
EQUALITY

CARE AND
EQUALITY

◆◇◆◇◆◇◆

INVENTING A NEW
FAMILY POLITICS

MONA HARRINGTON

ALFRED A. KNOPF
NEW YORK
1999

THIS IS A BORZOI BOOK
PUBLISHED BY ALFRED A. KNOPF, INC.

Copyright © 1999 by Mona Harrington
All rights reserved under International and Pan-American
Copyright Conventions. Published in the United States by
Alfred A. Knopf, Inc., New York, and simultaneously in
Canada by Random House of Canada Limited, Toronto.
Distributed by Random House, Inc., New York.

www.randomhouse.com

Knopf, Borzoi Books, and the colophon are registered
trademarks of Random House, Inc.

Library of Congress Cataloging-in-Publication Data
Harrington, Mona, [date]
Care and equality : inventing a new family
politics / Mona Harrington. — 1st ed.
p.   cm.
Includes index.
ISBN 0-375-40015-X
1. Family policy—Political aspects—United States.
2. Child welfare—Government policy—United States.
3. Child care—Government policy—United States.
4. Aged—Care—United States. 5. Aged—Government
policy—United States. 6. Women's rights—
United States. 7. United States—Social policy.
8. United States—Politics and government. I. Title.
HQ536.H325   1999
362.82'0973—dc21   98-43233   CIP

Manufactured in the United States of America
First Edition

To the memory of my mother,
Alice Payne Harrington,
whose voice is echoing in these pages

CONTENTS

Acknowledgments   ix

PROLOGUE: A CAST OF CHARACTERS IN A DRAMA OF THE '90S:
*Bill Clinton, Zoë Baird, Joycelyn Elders, Hillary Clinton,
Lani Guinier . . .   3*

PART ONE: TAKING CARE SERIOUSLY

CHAPTER 1:   *The Care-Equality Problem Enters Politics   11*
CHAPTER 2:   *A Collapsing Care System   25*
CHAPTER 3:   *Care as a National Political Value   44*

PART TWO: EMBRACING THE FAMILY

CHAPTER 4:   *Moral Panic: Sex, Families, Politics   63*
CHAPTER 5:   *Social Morality and Liberal Family Values   80*

PART THREE: ADDING IN EQUALITY

CHAPTER 6:   *Equal Authority: The Motherhood Problem   101*
CHAPTER 7:   *Equal Authority: The Warrior Problem   119*
CHAPTER 8:   *Equal Opportunity: The Problem of Private Authority   138*

PART FOUR: OPENING NEW POLITICAL CHANNELS

CHAPTER 9:   *A Break in the Order   159*
CHAPTER 10:   *A New Politics of Conversation   176*

Notes   189
Index   199

ACKNOWLEDGMENTS

THIS IS A BOOK ABOUT families, and it has involved my family from the beginning. My now adult children, Liza, Ben, and Thomas Gagnon, have read, talked about, and offered good criticism of the work at its various stages—and provided good companionship at every stage, even from afar. Paul Gagnon read every draft with uncommon patience, and, as always, stood by.

My long-standing reader-friends Nadya Aisenberg, Gillian Gill, Tom Butler, and Judith Nies helped me get started and well under way. A continuous conversation with Molly Shanley has been invaluable, her work on new family law and mine on a new family politics developing in tandem. Deborah Stone, Sara Chapman, and Lisa Dodson have read and offered careful commentary on key chapters. Kim Glickman, as a student at the Kennedy School, helped with research and also combed through the manuscript with a critical eye. Carolyn Killea, Sheila Statlender, Lynn Magee, Carole Shapiro, Ann Congleton, Margaret Sitko, and Laura Tommasi will recognize in the book ideas that they have passed on to me. My editor, Jane Garrett, has stood behind this project every step of the way. My agent, Charlotte Sheedy, has supplied spirit-sustaining praise, along with wise caution. And the Radcliffe Public Policy Institute, with its strong focus on issues of work and family, has provided a wonderfully supportive environment for the completion of the book.

CARE AND
EQUALITY

A CAST OF CHARACTERS
IN A DRAMA OF THE '90s:

Bill Clinton, Zoë Baird, Joycelyn Elders,
Hillary Clinton, Lani Guinier . . .

IN THE EARLY MONTHS OF 1999, Bill Clinton, who had won the presidency six years before with a heady promise of social renewal, stood before the nation shaken by a sex scandal and an impeachment trial. But the reform energies that had first swept him into office had dwindled long before that.

For me, the moment that graphically marked the end of initial hopes for change occurred one morning in September 1996. Glancing casually at the *New York Times,* coffee in hand, I was startled to see pictures of Peter Edelman and Mary Jo Bane beside the lead headline, which read, "Two Clinton Aides Resign to Protest New Welfare Law." The subheads went on: "Split in Administration: Top Officials Fault Approach Taken in Plan to End Aid Guarantee to Children."

The circle has closed, I thought. We're back at the beginning.

What came to mind was a summer weekend ten years before when the same cast of characters had been present at a gathering of political activists and academics meeting to plan the advancement of a liberal agenda. It was in August 1986, on Martha's Vineyard, at a large summer home overlooking what seemed like miles of unsullied beach and ocean. A Cambridge couple, long engaged in liberal causes, had invited about fifty people from a variety of fields—politics, health care, entertainment, law—to discuss ways of creating a new sense of national responsibility for social issues. In the middle of the Reagan years, how could liberals combat the reigning conservative orthodoxy, the tax-cutting, the deregulating, and the devolving of power to the states? How could they persuade Americans that truly open opportunity—wide access to good health care, good housing, good education, good employment—required careful national monitoring of the country's giant economy? How could they promote the liberal dream of a shared-by-all responsibility for keeping the American promise of freedom and equality alive for all the country's people?

Peter Edelman, a Georgetown law professor, and Marian Wright Edelman, head of the Children's Defense Fund, were at the Vineyard meeting as longtime social activists. Mary Jo Bane, then a professor at the Kennedy School of Government at Harvard, was there as an expert on welfare issues and a critic of the welfare systems then in place. Bill and Hillary Clinton were there as liberal political practitioners—he was then governor of Arkansas. (They left the meetings for a while one afternoon to attend the wedding of a friend somewhere on the island. The friend, I realized long afterward, must have been Lani Guinier.) I was there because I had just published *The Dream of Deliverance in American Politics,*[1] a book about a deeply rooted political myth that sets up chronic resistance in Americans to broad public responsibility for social ills. Except for the Clintons, it was a meeting of political outsiders, critics cheerfully defying the odds against overcoming the conservative spirit of the times.

Then six years later, in 1992, liberal fortunes took an incredible turn. Bill Clinton was elected president, and a whole cadre of people with hopes for a renewed social consciousness in the country went to Washington with him. Mary Jo Bane became cochair of a group designing a new national welfare policy. Peter Edelman became an assistant secretary of health and human services. Hillary Clinton assembled a vast network of consultants to design a comprehensive national health care policy. Lani Guinier was nominated to head the Justice Department's Civil Rights Division. Women, blacks, and other minorities entered national office in unprecedented numbers. Problems of poverty, race, equality, health, education—the deepening social troubles of the country—had finally emerged from the Reagan blackout onto the *national* agenda.

But the liberal program of the new Clinton administration barely had a chance to develop before it began to collapse, to fragment, to lose its coherence. First came a series of political explosions starting even before Bill Clinton took office and continuing relentlessly into his presidency. Gays in the military. Zoë Baird and illegal immigrant nannies. Lani Guinier and race quotas. Somalia and United Nations peace forces. Health care, big government, and Hillary. Haiti and Jimmy Carter. Joycelyn Elders, condoms, masturbation. Bosnia. Each new issue called down charges of everything from ignorance and incompetence to arrogance and decadence.

And then there was the slow erosion of the major policy initiatives and the big defeats. Facing an epic budget battle, the administration abandoned an early plan for a national jobs program. The ambitious proposal for universal health insurance engineered by Hillary Clinton hit fierce opposition by the industries affected and ultimately died in the midst of heated congressional wrangles. In this hostile atmosphere, the administration did not even submit to the Congress its plan for restructuring welfare with generous supports for working parents. Finally, the election of 1994 overturned long-standing Democratic majorities in both the House and Senate.

That seemed the end of liberal hope for many. But Bane and Edelman, among others, hung on, aiming at least to block the Republican Congress from dismantling policies already in place. And they did successfully urge presidential vetoes of two Republican welfare bills that drastically reduced supports for poor families. Then came the ultimate blow. Bill Clinton, in the midst of the 1996 presidential campaign, signed into law, as the *Times* reported, a welfare package that was not so draconian as the earlier Republican plans, but nonetheless ended national guarantees of support for the poor—a policy that dated back to the New Deal. So Bane and Edelman quit. Hope for strong national social policies, hope nurtured by an ardent corps of reformers through years of research, writing, meeting, lobbying, fund-raising, and campaigning for liberal politicians was, once more, crushed.

The pressing question is: Why did this happen? Why were liberals unable to enact the major pieces of their program when they seemed to have a good chance—under a president who had worked with them for years and who had made them a part of his administration? An even more interesting question looks to the future. Where do liberals go from here—assuming, as I do, that liberalism is not dead?

Answers to these questions depend on a close rereading of the early '90s when Bill Clinton took office. This was a point when deep trouble in the country's social order was pushing into public view new and complicated issues that liberals were peculiarly ill equipped to handle. And yet, paradoxically, they were issues that liberals themselves, without recognizing the full significance of what they were dealing with, had generated and nurtured through the decades. When the Clinton liberals arrived in Washington, then, they were met by a fractious genie that they and their forebears had unwittingly released.

At the core of the new trouble was radical change in the status of American women. Driven both by economic need and by renewed claims to equality, unprecedented numbers of women began a migration in the 1960s out of the home and into the paid workplace. And liberals had been champions of this change—champions of equality and champions of the right of individuals to choose how to live their lives. Liberal writers had contributed crucially to the shift in traditional ideas about women's place, undermining the automatic assignment of women to homemaking. Liberal activists had struggled to clear away a maze of written and unwritten restrictions that had, for generations, kept women who did work outside the home segregated in domestic, clerical, nursing, or teaching jobs. By the 1980s, it was no longer remarkable to see women in medicine, or law, or the military, or politics, or the construction trades. By the 1990s, the full-time, lifetime homemaker had become a rarity, and the woman at work—in jobs of all kinds, at all income levels—was an established fact of national life.

But the new work patterns, while opening opportunity for women, were also producing disturbing and disorienting effects. Unwarned and unprepared, Americans were facing deep disruption in the country's family structures, its systems of caretaking, its codes of sexual morality, and its conception of sexual equality in the workplace, in public life, and in the home.

The litany of trouble wound through this social upheaval is all too familiar: high rates of divorce, single-parent households with low incomes giving rise to the sad pathologies of poverty, two-income households with little parental time for children, schools overwhelmed with the need to become surrogate parents, courts swamped by children and adolescents in trouble, elders without family or community supports, marriages and families all across the social scale stressed by long work hours, women torn between the demands of the workplace and the needs of families at home, and—perhaps most unnerving—the old romantic war between the sexes hardened into conflict along new lines marked by new meanings to words like discrimination, affirmative action, harassment, abuse, domestic violence, and rape.

This is the juncture—or disjuncture—where the liberal imagination that shaped the reforms of the 1930s and the 1960s falls short of the present challenge.

In the past, mainstream liberal programs focused on threats or injustices stemming from two sources of danger to ordinary Americans: business, holding the power to exploit economic weakness; and government, holding the power to override individual freedoms. In the New Deal, liberals used government to restrain and regulate business. In Lyndon Johnson's War on Poverty, they tried to subsidize enough education and housing and health care and small-business start-ups to boost the poor into the middle class. And throughout, liberal lawyers have kept vigilant watch for abuses of civil rights.

But intensely absorbed with questions of economic justice and individual rights, liberals have never formed a clear social theory that connects individuals, economics, and families. Nor have they looked squarely at the tortuous implications of moving women from the separate sphere of the home to a position of full, meaningful equality.

Specifically, there is no mainstream liberal program that measures the economics of caretaking for the whole country, that charts the distribution of caretaking work, that assigns weight to care as a value defining national goals, that takes a stand on the importance of family as a source of care, that speaks to the moral dimension of families as a social unit, or that even begins to recognize the ways in which women's equality is bound up with the organization of families and care. There is, in short, no mainstream liberal politics of the family.

When Bill Clinton entered the White House in 1993, therefore, the stage was set for political crisis. Liberals he appointed carried into office with them the whole range of projects that they had tirelessly discussed and elaborated while out of power. It was Mary Jo Bane, for example, who with her Harvard colleague David Ellwood brought sophisticated planning for new welfare subsidies to move poor single mothers into the workforce on good competitive terms. Joycelyn Elders brought educational and medical programs to combat teen pregnancy. Both Clintons and their many activist friends were firmly determined, in the name of equality, to increase the numbers of minorities and women in the cabinet, in the courts, and in other high governmental positions. But, without a clear sense of the swarm of linked issues surrounding any matter involving sex, motherhood, family, caretaking, or women's rights, the Clinton liberals did not grasp the depth of trouble they were touching with even their most moderate social proposals. And, one after another, their initiatives detonated political explosions that threw the new administration into continuing crisis—and tossed the liberals in it, once more, out of power.

What I propose to do here is to trace the course of the early explosions and their aftermath to locate the literal point where the absence of a liberal family politics derails its best hopes. And I propose also to outline, broadly, what such a new liberal family politics might look like.

THE STORY STARTS on the first day of the first Clinton administration, when the president has just been sworn in and is sitting down to lunch, and the inaugural parade is forming to begin its triumphal progress down Pennsylvania Avenue. Behind the public scene, Senator Joseph Biden, Democratic chair of the Judiciary Committee, has waylaid the president to warn him of a serious problem concerning his nominee for attorney general, Zoë Baird.

PART ONE

TAKING CARE
SERIOUSLY

CHAPTER I

THE CARE-EQUALITY PROBLEM ENTERS POLITICS

Years now after the event, I can still see Zoë Baird leaning toward the microphone before the Senate Judiciary Committee, eyes puffy, mouth tight, trying to be understood, explaining again and again why she had hired illegal aliens as nanny and chauffeur, and why she had not paid Social Security taxes on them, while she worked in the top managerial ranks of the Aetna Insurance Company—and why this should not bar her appointment to the office of attorney general.

Baird was a forty-year-old lawyer who had worked briefly in the Justice Department and a big Washington law firm before turning to in-house corporate work and rising quickly to become general counsel at Aetna. This, like most high positions in the legal profession, was a demanding job, requiring long and unpredictable work hours. The rest of the picture follows the familiar pattern etched by the experience of working women throughout the country. Baird was the mother of a small child. Her husband also worked long hours. They needed extensive child care.

But here Baird's story differed from that of most families. She had a stunningly high income—$500,000 a year—which allowed hiring a couple to provide domestic help on a full-time, live-in basis. Nonetheless, Baird told the committee, she and her husband had had difficulty finding such help, particularly a qualified live-in nanny, which is why they had ended up hiring immigrants who had entered the country illegally. Then they had made the mistake—following legal advice, she said—of not paying Social Security taxes while proceedings to legalize their employees' status were under way.

Bill Clinton, as president-elect, announced Baird's nomination for attorney general with his last batch of cabinet selections on Christmas Eve 1992, fulfilling pledges to have his cabinet set before Christmas and to have it "look like America," with the faces of women and minorities breaking up the usual array of white males. He was not concerned about the irregularities in Baird's home-help arrangements, which she had disclosed as soon as she had become a serious candidate. Everyone involved with the cabinet selections had thought the matter would be resolved when Baird straightened out the tax question, which her lawyers were doing.

But when Senator Biden, as Judiciary Committee chair, reviewed Baird's record in preparation for her confirmation hearings, alarm bells went off. What Biden feared was an outburst of populist resentment against the wealthy who lived as if bothersome laws did not apply to them. This was the message he had conveyed to the newly sworn-in president in the midst of inauguration festivities—to no immediate avail. The matter still did not seem highly serious to the Clinton staff.

In spite of his forebodings, then, Biden began the hearings on January 19, the day before the inauguration, and they resumed on the twenty-first, only to end, ignominiously, late that night. In the meantime, a sudden deluge of phone calls had poured in to the Senate and to radio talk shows all around the country by people outraged about Baird and the nanny.

It was one of those occasions like the Anita Hill–Clarence Thomas exchange—also before the Judiciary Committee—when a public issue suddenly touched off a high-voltage emotional charge. Newspapers were flooded with commentary. Discussions flared up everywhere, with people speaking passionately on all sides of the question. At a business lunch, a woman I did not know well suddenly and tearfully poured out a story about hiring illegal help herself when she was desperate to find at-home care for her dying mother. She couldn't afford the going rate for regular round-the-clock nursing, and her other choices were to leave her mother in a nursing home where care proved unreliable, or to quit her job and try to nurse her mother herself. Later she learned that her nearly helpless mother would have been eligible for a higher level of nursing-home care had her illness been correctly diagnosed. Serious physical and mental debilitation had been ascribed to Alzheimer's disease; an autopsy revealed a brain tumor. Since that information came tragically late, the solution had been to hire an illegal alien, a trained nurse who, without a green card, had no choice but to take live-in work at lower-than-standard nursing wages.

In another gathering, when I was defending Baird as stuck in a tangle of bad choices, a friend exploded in anger precisely over the issue of caretakers without choices, the issue of exploitation. This was a black woman, a college professor, and she recalled furiously the generations of black women who served as live-in help in white homes because they, like illegal aliens, had few alternatives. "We won't do that anymore!" she shouted. "And no one else should have to do it either!" She added that she never even hired cleaning help, "because no one else should have to clean up my dirt." I argued that dirt isn't the problem; you can go to work and leave it there, which you can't do with kids. But she wasn't really arguing about dirt. She was arguing about inequality and injustice. And she had no sympathy for Zoë Baird and others in her position who were handing *their* work off to other, less fortunate women.

If I was taken aback by the reaction of friends and acquaintances, senators who had to go on record for or against Zoë Baird were appalled. The instant public reaction, the anger, the volume of calls, their ubiquitousness, moved one after another to quick declarations of non-support for her appointment. It all ended when Baird asked the president to withdraw her nomination in a hastily drafted exchange of letters released to the press at 1:30 a.m. on January 22.

The intensity of popular reaction to what was immediately dubbed Nannygate was remarkable, but the more so as Bill Clinton and his transition team were completely blindsided by it. Senator Biden had expected trouble, but even he, on the evidence of his public remarks, did not grasp the depth of the problem that Baird represented.

A telling moment in this whole story is the point at which Senator Biden talked to President Clinton at the inauguration lunch. These two men were Democrats. Both stood somewhere—not very far out, but somewhere—in the liberal wing of their party. Clinton, after all, had expressed his liberal allegiances by deliberately opening up high office to groups previously excluded from power by sex or race. Biden and Clinton together, conferring at lunch, were looking at the same set of facts: the nominee for attorney general had broken immigration laws by hiring undocumented workers to take care of her child and household, and had broken Social Security tax laws, apparently to protect the workers against deportation. But looking at these facts, each man saw different things. Biden saw class conflict. Clinton, we have to assume from his lack of alarm, saw a commonplace situation—laws so widely broken under the pressure of great demand for scarce domestic help that neither immigration nor tax officials paid much attention to the issue. For him, it was a technicality.

What neither man could see, because it wasn't there, was a liberal frame for the problem in front of them. They could not see its full contours or its seriousness. They had no idea that when Zoë Baird walked into the Senate committee room, she carried with her, simply in who she was, a set of conflicts, layered and compacted, that were pushing their way into every corner of the society.

At one point in her brief moment before the committee, Baird, when asked how she, as a lawyer, could have taken employment laws so lightly, replied, "I guess I was thinking more as a mother than a lawyer." There it was. As a working mother, she had to arrange care for her young child. As a lawyer working extraordinarily long hours, she needed live-in help. When she had trouble finding it, she turned to the illegal labor market—immigrants illegally in the country, illegally in the workforce. The mother and the lawyer were in conflict. The lawyer and the law were in conflict. The immigrant workers and the law were in conflict. Senator Biden and President Clinton were in conflict. And, very quickly, the nominee and millions of Americans were in conflict.

These conflicts ended the possibility of Baird becoming the country's first woman attorney general. And not only Baird. Bill Clinton's next choice for the office was Kimba Wood, a federal district court judge in New York. She was, on paper, actually a better candidate than Baird, due to wider legal experience. But she, too, had young children. And she, too, it turned out, had a nanny who had entered the country illegally.

Initially, Wood told the White House that she did not have a Zoë Baird problem. What she meant, but did not at first explain, was that when she had hired her undocumented nanny, it was not illegal to do so. And she had scrupulously paid all applicable taxes. In other words, she interpreted the "problem" as breaking the law, which, literally, she had not done. The White House had learned, however, that whatever the problem was, it went beyond the letter of the law. The whole subject of aliens, or nannies, or high-salaried women, or something was a political hot potato, and the Wood nomination was quickly dropped.

With Zoë Baird and Kimba Wood, the care-equality-family problem had entered American politics. And yet, given its unfamiliarity and the continuing turmoil in the unseasoned Clinton White House, the problem as a complicated whole remained unseen and undefined politically.

What politicans and commentators and ordinary people calling in to talk shows did see took two basic forms. Radio, TV, newspapers, and magazines carried countless condemnations of Baird, expressing the class resentments that Senator Biden had identified. She was exploiting low-wage help and cheating on taxes on a salary of $500,000 a year! And why did she hire foreigners with so many Americans out of work? She could get good help if she were willing to pay for it. Then there was the choice she had made between work and family. Why was she holding a job that required such long hours that she needed live-in help in the first place? Why didn't she stay at home and take care of her young child herself! The problem was wrongdoing.

Reactions from working women sympathetic to Baird and Wood were equally intense and angry. No male candidate in his confirmation hearings had ever been asked about the legal status of his household help! The Senate was running a double standard in holding this kind of illegality against women alone.

The sole substantive response to this uproar was to cast the nanny problem as gender neutral. Men, too, would be asked about their compliance with immigration and tax laws concerning the people they employed. The result was a flurry of lawyer consulting and tax paying among would-be federal officials. Then Congress devised yet a further solution. In October 1994, the Social Security Domestic Employment Reform Act became law and made life easier for employers of home help by reducing the categories of employees on whom taxes must be paid in the first place.

But as the political system responded in a kind of panic to this string of mini-crises, the totality of the social problem producing them remained incomprehensible to the officials and analysts who move questions into public debate. They did not grasp that they were watching an increasingly fragile caretaking structure moving toward collapse. They did not see a massive collision occurring between the country's need for caretaking and the ancient American promise of equality. They did not perceive that they themselves were actors in a social and political tradition at odds with unstoppable social change under way.

For liberals, the problem was that they could pick up class issues readily, as Senator Biden did, but gender issues remained baffling. Oddly, however, Bill Clinton's blankness on the matter, his failure to see that the nanny issue would be explosive, represents some implicit movement in liberal thought. In all probability, he did not see trouble ahead because the circles he inhabited were full of hardworking professional women, including, most notably, his mother and his wife. The choices of these women, their struggles with family care and the whole range of work-family issues, were familiar and sympathy-evoking facts of life to him. In other words, Clinton missed the class issue because, in advance of many liberals, he was focusing on the gender issue.

But, unfortunately for him, for Baird, for her nanny, for liberals, for women, and for the country generally, he was not focusing on the *whole* gender issue. What he missed was the troubling two-sided connection between women's equality and the problem of caretaking.

Within long-standing American tradition, the mechanism for advancing equality for all, beyond the basic political rights of citizenship, was open and equal opportunity in the marketplace. Also within long and revered tradition, the society's caretaking function—child care, elder care, family care of all kinds—depended on the unpaid labor of women at home. But if women were doing their work at home, they could not participate in the market, except marginally, and couldn't seek equality there. In other words, historically, the promise of equality did not apply to women.

This is the history that the revitalized women's movement of the 1970s challenged vigorously. Women would claim equal opportunity in the marketplace and complete the mission begun by the suffragists of the nineteenth century whose long labors won women the vote. And, of course, American women, whether in search of equality or simply of income, have been pouring into the paid workplace ever since. But while working women are on the job, they are, obviously, not at home taking care of families. And, increasingly, neither are their mothers, or aunts, or grandmothers—the backup caretakers of earlier years—as these women too are likely to be out at work.

The problem, the enormous problem for Americans in the 1990s, is that we have not devised any equality-respecting system to replace the full-time caretaking labor force of women at home. We have patch-work systems, but we have come nowhere near replacing the hours or the quality of care that the at-home women of previous generations provided for the country. And the social ills that follow from this incalculable loss of care are all too familiar. I recited that sad litany earlier.

But the other piece of the story is that women's remaining caretaking responsibilities undermine their equal opportunity in the work world. A still-strong social ethic assigns these responsibilities primarily to women, not to men. And most women, but not most men, compromise their time at work somewhere along the line in order to spend time at home with their families. In a work world that values employees precisely in terms of time, women then fall behind their male colleagues in all measures of reward and advancement.

Statistics tell the familiar story. Women's wages lower than men's. Women clustered in lower levels of most workplaces. Top corporate management 95 percent male. In the professions, only 10 to 15 percent of top positions filled by women. Even with recent gains, only a tiny minority of women in Congress or in governorships.

These are the statistics that Bill and Hillary Clinton, and their enthusiastic backers in women's rights organizations, had in mind in their determination to appoint a significant number of women to the cabinet and to other official positions. But here the plague of confusions surrounding the concept of women's equality came into play, causing trouble for the president-elect as soon as his transition team started its work.

The first, set deeply in American history and in mainstream liberal principle, is that there is no unambiguous concept of women's equality, as such. The principle to be honored and protected politically is *individual* equality. If women were excluded from medical schools, or law firms, or juries, or social clubs, if political parties were not backing them for stepping-stone offices that led to governorships or to Congress, the principle being offended was individual equality. Women were not being judged on individual merit. They were being judged on the basis of stereotypical ideas about the nature of women as a sex. It was when women's advocates in the '60s raised this argument in clear terms that the most egregious barriers to women in the workplace and in public life began to fall. The powerful idea of fairness to the individual was the lever that made the difference.

Bill Clinton, however, in promoting his female appointees, was not entirely protected by the individual equality principle. In proclaiming that he would significantly extend the presence of women in important federal offices, he was safely within the bounds of individual rights as long as he could maintain that their absence in previous years was due to a disregard for individual merit. But he could do that only by making it clear that his appointments *were* based on merit and not on sex, as such. If he appeared to be playing a numbers game—so many women, so many minorities—he was standing on ground other than that sanctified by dearly held American tradition. And he would also be departing from the strongly defended liberal tradition of individual rights.

That departure is exactly what seemed to be under way, and it provoked a drumbeat of criticism—which in turn provoked a Clinton defense, setting off a further round of criticism. The problem was whether or not to choose a woman candidate for attorney general who had a track record of involvement in women's issues and who would, presumably, promote them once in office.

The first strong candidate, Brooksley Born, a Washington lawyer active in women's affairs, was enthusiastically backed by women's organizations, especially those with well-established headquarters and networks in Washington. But Bill Clinton, concerned about criticism that he was paying off interest groups rather than seeking merit, and annoyed by the charge from activists that he was appointing too *few* women, ruled Born out of contention and countercriticized the women's groups as "bean counters."

Zoë Baird then became the front-runner precisely because she had had no involvement with women's issues. She was, as is commonly said in these circumstances, simply a lawyer "who happened to be a woman." In other words, she stood as a candidate chosen not as a representative of women but as a meritorious professional. However, the problem here was that, compared with potential male candidates for the top legal job in the country, Baird's merit was not outstanding. She was young, only fifteen years out of law school. Virtually all of her experience was in corporate law. Although she had worked at the Justice Department for a short time early in her career, she had no significant background in law enforcement or the judiciary. She was, in fact, chosen because she was a woman.

Clinton, therefore, while trying to stay on the safe side of the merit principle, ended up outside it, but without taking an open stand justifying such a move. His problem was that to do so, he would have had to rely on a way of thinking about equality and equal rights that the liberal mainstream had not firmly accepted—and that conservatives of all hues adamantly rejected. He would have had to argue that it was important to bring women, as women, into important positions in government because their long exclusion had resulted in the exclusion of the varied ideas and perspectives and judgments that women's experience of life produced, and that men in office had long ignored.

Women's physical vulnerability, for example, to rape and domestic violence was a problem that an all-male justice system had always treated as far less serious than it actually was. But, by 1992, it was possible to point to the fact that women lawyers and judges had brought into their profession perspectives that had produced significant and needed change in laws on violence against women. In other arenas similar changes were occurring: women doctors were bringing women's health issues—notably breast cancer—into public notice; women in the labor movement were organizing to raise concerns about primarily female workplaces. In short, throughout the country, women's voices were bringing different, important, and previously unheard messages to public attention. An argument that the president should act deliberately to include such voices in his cabinet—that he *should* appoint women as women—could rest on this record.

But Bill Clinton could not make such an argument without departing from established liberal thought and adopting what was still an outsider position—one pressed by feminists and racial minorities, groups that had not been part of the national political conversation historically. Further, he would have been teetering dangerously on the edge of a position with a worrisome downside.

In the past, it was precisely group identification that had worked *against* women, blacks, Asians, Jews, Catholics, and other supposed inferiors, and it was the persistent claim to individual rights that had protected them. Therefore, liberals, as champions of the disadvantaged, hesitated to tinker with the claims of the individual and had not developed a solid, widely accepted stand incorporating the idea of group representation in government into its portfolio of principles.

This fact—the absence of a liberal principle recognizing group perspectives and voices as a means of moving the unequal toward equality—became dramatically clear soon afterward in the controversy over Lani Guinier, which I discuss in chapter 9. But without such a principle in place, Bill Clinton had no firm ground to stand on to defend his attorney general candidate except individual merit measured by professional credentials, and as already noted, his candidate had a credentials problem—before even reaching the nanny problem.

But the nanny problem, the one that Senator Biden saw as a matter of class and Bill Clinton didn't see at all, is at the heart of the matter. It directly connects the complications of equality—group identity, group perspective, professional credentials—and the complications of care. And it also marks out a yawning absence in the liberal stance on women's equality.

Zoë Baird would not have been even a plausible candidate for attorney general if she had not held such a position as general counsel of a major corporation. But she would not have held such a position if she had not thrown herself into the work of a fast-paced lawyer on the same terms as her male colleagues—which meant, in the business culture that came to dominate the legal profession in the 1980s—time demands that could easily reach twelve hours a day or more.

That, of course, explains why Zoë Baird needed a nanny. And as most professional women leave the fast track at some point, it also explains why there were relatively few in the pool of plausible candidates for attorney general—or for any high office. The upshot is that the rules for inclusion in the country's important places of authority—individual merit measured by conventionally recognized credentials—effectively exclude most women as women.

But the equality problem is not confined to professional women. It winds inextricably around the care problem generally, and both run straight across class lines. Most women earning middle-range incomes cannot afford as much caretaking as their families need, and they compensate by racing between job and home to provide as much family care as possible themselves. Or they work part-time or flextime. But workers limiting time on the job, by whatever arrangement, tend to remain at the lower levels of their occupations. And since women are mainly the ones doing this, their choices—which are entirely reasonable and humane—are reinforcing the old pattern of women's work ghettoes.

Women in low-wage jobs are worse off yet, as they simply cannot pay for adequate family care. Except where increasingly limited public subsidies are available, the result too often is entrapment of all family members in a downward spiral that makes the promise of equal opportunity a cruel joke.

Sadly, care workers themselves generally fall into this last category. Desperate need on the part of families at all income levels creates a huge market demand for care. But, as most people who need day care or elder care have limited resources to pay for it, wage levels for caretaking remain low, and the supply of care workers depends on people who have no choice but to take low-paid jobs. As a result, we are headed toward hardening inequality in the creation of a new, low-wage servant class to do our caretaking for us.

Further, as the Zoë Baird story illustrates, the main source of low-wage service labor is immigration—both legal and illegal and largely Hispanic. Depending on these workers, we create not just a servant class but one made up of racial and ethnic minorities who, in large part, do not have the power—often not even the right to vote—to improve their employment conditions politically.

Whether or not Baird's particular troubles were her own fault, whether or not she had better choices than she made, her appearance on the political stage and its swift ending mark an undeniable dilemma:

in spite of the fact that most American women are in the paid work-force, we have not taken full account of what that means. We are operating as if they were still at home much of the time taking care of their families.

And here is yet another layer of complication in this long story. It is clear from the tenor of personal and political talk about families that some strong sense remains among Americans that women *should* be at home much of the time taking care of family life.

Bolstering this belief is the remaining power of the idea that women have a natural capacity for the care of children and others, and that these natural gifts make it right, not simply convenient, for the woman of the family to provide, or oversee, its care. Whether this idea stems from moral conviction, or personal observation, or emotional longing for the securities of a simpler time, it clouds recognition of the fact that the women of the country are not at home and are not going home—at least not on the old terms.

In a final twist, the idea of women's natural caretaking qualities has another powerful effect that was also at play, I believe, in the Zoë Baird affair. If women are good at the emotional work of caring for others, it follows, for many people, that they are not good at work that depends on disciplined rationality and toughness—like law. I have explored this set of attitudes at length in a book on women lawyers,[1] finding that the legal profession, prizing combativeness in argument and strict objectivity in judgment, long resisted accepting the women in its ranks as equals and generally relegated them to the lower levels of practice.

The stereotyping that informs this outlook has been under challenge long enough to have lost some force, but the spectacle of a woman attorney general still had the capacity to shock. Before the Clinton presidency, no woman had ever held one of the power positions in the cabinet—secretary of state, or defense, or of the treasury, or attorney general—all of which have traditionally called for unalloyed masculine traits. The ideal attorney general, both superlawyer and supercop, would combine the cool, steely, steady rationality of the lawyer and the tough aggressiveness of the enforcer. And time-honored images of the admirable woman—emotional, intuitive, sympathetic, generous, deferential, cooperative—simply do not fit the top-lawyer ideal.

Most working women will recognize this catch-22, and recognize also that it is another equality block. If a woman is not tough and forceful, she is not qualified for top jobs; if she *is* as tough and forceful as her male colleagues, she is off-putting and not suitable for top jobs. This is the natural-caretaker concept operating in the workplace.

Missing in this equality-blocking box of stereotypes, however, is the idea that someone who *is* caring, who understands caretaking, who knows its importance, and who recognizes a current caretaking crisis would be a highly valuable decision maker in government or the private sector.

And this idea circles back to the question of whether liberals should think about the deliberate inclusion of women as women in decision-making because they bring a perspective that has been missing in national life. Nature has not designed all women as empathic caretakers, no matter how comforting it is to think so. But most women, due to the social rules that assign responsibility for care, have more experience of that responsibility than most men have. Excluding women from equal participation in the country's decision-making effectively excludes much knowledge and experience of the care question.

This is not to say that all women think alike on social issues. Conservative women are as adamant as conservative men in resisting broadened public responsibility for work-family problems and caretaking generally. But that is not a reason for liberals to be squeamish about deliberately adding women's experience to the public debate, and making the logic of this position clear.

Perhaps Zoë Baird, with little prior involvement in women's issues, would not have carried the care question into the cabinet with her. But the adage that you can never tell was borne out in fairly short order by the conduct in office of the attorney general Bill Clinton was finally able to appoint.

In Janet Reno, he had a nominee who, as a woman, advanced the equal rights agenda but who, as an older, unmarried woman without children, did not provoke the nation's volatile tensions about mothers and care. And as a longtime state's attorney in Florida—a prosecutor, an enforcer—she passed the toughness test. Therefore, although female, she was an acceptable candidate for the top-lawyer role, traditionally defined. Or so it seemed.

What the country learned only after her confirmation was that her true passion as a prosecutor of wrongdoers was to right the wrong of inadequate child care! The story behind most criminal records, she firmly believed, was poor care, especially in early childhood. And this is the message she began to carry in speech after speech around the country: put public money behind supports for the care of children.

BUT THE LARGER QUESTION of putting the need for new systems of family care together with meaningful support for women's equality continued to elude the Clinton administration and liberals generally. To be sure, such a project would mean rewriting a long history in which caretaking depended on inequality, but the country was founded on a rewriting of history. This is what Americans do. More specifically, this is what American liberals do—and need to do in order to support these two difficult, basic values, because our present systems do *not* support them.

CHAPTER 2

A COLLAPSING
CARE SYSTEM

Two weeks after the hurried departure of Zoë Baird from the public scene, Bill Clinton enjoyed an upbeat moment in his encounters with the issue of care. On Friday, February 5, 1993, he signed into law the Family and Medical Leave Act, which guaranteed workers twelve weeks of unpaid leave to care for newborn or newly adopted children, or close relatives suffering serious illness. This was the first bill he signed as president, and with the winter sun shining, he marked the occasion with a Rose Garden ceremony.

But the triumph was not unclouded. Just the night before, the White House staff, preparing to go ahead with Kimba Wood for attorney general, learned of Wood's hard-to-explain nanny arrangement and backed off the nomination. Wood reacted by hastily announcing the withdrawal of her candidacy, and that irresistible story led the Friday news. The media gave family leave, and the president as its champion, only a passing glance.

The crossed wires, the frustrations, the disappointments of that day could stand as a metaphor for the troubles with family care besetting the country generally. We don't "see" the problem. We don't see a collapsing care system because we don't see care as a system to begin with. We see individuals making private decisions about who takes care of the children or helps an arthritis-plagued elderly parent. We see families using the private market for services they don't have time to provide themselves—day care, housecleaning, fast food. We don't add all of this up and call it a system that is working well or badly.

When things go wrong, when a mother leaves children alone because she cannot afford day care while she works, when marriages fail under the stress of job and family demands, when unsupervised teenagers in cities *and* suburbs turn to sex and drugs, we generally see specific problems—moral, economic—but not an entire care system in trouble.

If we did see systemic collapse, we would have to start thinking about care as it affects the workings of the whole society. We would have to start seeing it as a matter of "the general Welfare" which we are charged by the Constitution to promote. We would have to start designing public policy supporting care in ways that we have never previously imagined—and, of course, I am proposing that we should.

What stands in the way, however, is the remaining hold—not absolute but still strong—of a political tradition that defines what we can rightly regard as public business and what we must respect as strictly private.

The very words "private" and "privacy" have a talismanic quality in American political life. Someone opposed to a government decision or proposal of any kind need just utter the magic words to raise an alarm and provoke debate. As Clinton himself put it after a year in office, "You know, this country got started by people who wanted a good letting alone from government. And every time we think of doing anything around here we have to recognize that Americans have always had a healthy skepticism about government reaching into their lives."[1]

The president, who was introducing his Supreme Court nominee, Stephen Breyer, was answering a question when he made that remark, not speaking from a script, and the unconstructed movement of his thought from the first to second sentence is worth noting. In the first he is referring to the shield the Bill of Rights provides for the ordinary citizen potentially threatened by a powerful government. We can't be executed, jailed, or fined without due process of law. We can't be forbidden to express our opinions in public. We can't be forbidden to terminate pregnancies, at least in their early stages. The boundary drawn here runs between government and the private lives of individuals. But the president's second sentence slips to a broader idea when he refers to the skepticism about government that surfaces "every time we think of doing anything around here."

It's not clear whether "here" is the White House or Washington, but in either case, he is talking about public policy, governmental programs setting up rules or systems with some fairly broad sweep.

The Family and Medical Leave Act itself is a clear case in point. It had taken eight years to pass what was, in its specific terms, a very modest bill. Admittedly, the federal government was imposing restrictions on business by prohibiting the firing of workers who take long leaves to deal with family needs. But the restrictions were far from onerous: they covered leaves only for certain specified purposes, the permitted leaves were relatively short *and* unpaid, and the law didn't apply to small business—which meant that it didn't apply to more than half of the nation's workers. Still, when Representative Patricia Schroeder of Colorado first introduced the bill in 1985, no one would join her in sponsoring it. When it was finally passed in 1990, President George Bush vetoed it, and he vetoed it again in 1992, acceding to the classic arguments against governmental interference in the private market.

Here was the ideology of private prerogatives making itself felt in American politics. Every other wealthy industrialized nation had long provided *paid* family leave for periods ranging from ten to seventy-two weeks. But in the United States, the concept of imposing public responsibilities on private business operations stands as a barrier that has to be contested issue by issue, and the burden of proof always lies with the claim of public need.

In this context, the Family and Medical Leave Act posed a special problem. It not only placed restrictions on private business, it justified those restrictions with the claim that the private family could not sustain its caretaking responsibilities on its own and needed public support. In other words, the family leave bill implicitly asserted a public interest in family care. But the problem with this claim was that the idea of the private family is, if anything, more sacrosanct in American tradition than the idea of private business. Therefore to justify restrictions on business by asserting family needs put the liberal backers of the bill on extremely shaky ground.

But the eight-year struggle over family leave proved to be just a skir-
mish in light of what was soon to come—a monumental two-year losing battle over national health care. The story of that battle is a maze of
complexity, and anyone who wants to trace the lines of its intricate
plots and subplots should read *The System: The American Way of Politics
at the Breaking Point* by journalists Haynes Johnson and David S.
Broder.[2] This is an extraordinary book, both for the depth and
throughness of its reporting and the clarity of its analysis. It is so thorough and clear, in fact, that at the end it is impossible to say what person or group or action or inaction killed the Clinton plan. The clash of
powerful parties on all sides of the issue produced chaotic deadlock.

But the large outlines of the conflict were clear enough. It was an
American special: a public versus private brawl. The Clintons, in the
public corner, sought to use governmental regulation and subsidies to
reorganize the country's health insurance system. The goal was to in-
sure everyone and to control the costs of care. In other words, the Clinton plan asserted the legitimacy of a public interest in the health of all
Americans, an interest serious enough to justify extensive governmental regulation of the private health care industries.

On the private side, various insurance companies, small-business
owners, hospitals, and medical groups protested that governmental involvement in the health care market would undermine good care and
bankrupt many companies required to pay for it. They were relying on
the basic ideology of private enterprise, the idea that the market working blindly through its internal natural logic produces the best possible
results for everyone—owner, manager, worker, consumer.

The problem for the Clinton administration was to justify its plan by
demonstrating a public need so clear and compelling that it would
overcome the private market claims. But here the Clintons ran into another privacy problem. With the question of health as with family care,
the claim of public interest implied a governmental interest in highly
private matters—in the case of health care, the relation between individuals and their doctors.

Initially the Clinton plan evoked widespread enthusiasm for the
idea that the government would guarantee health insurance to everyone. In other words, it would enhance the control individuals would
have over their own well-being. But under claims by the health care

industries that the plan would prevent people from choosing their own doctors and would limit access to expensive kinds of treatment, public support crumbled. Then it looked as if making health a public rather than a private responsibility would result in a loss of control over personal welfare. It looked like a dangerous, not a benign, governmental intrusion into private affairs. In fact, it evoked fears that for the government to be involved in anything personal, anything private, was always dangerous.

But even the ferocious contest over health care did not reveal the full scale of the ongoing argument among Americans over where the boundary should lie between public and private matters. That awaited the debate over welfare.

The question here was whether or not poor people should be entitled to public support, as they had been since the first extensive welfare program was established during the New Deal. Bill Clinton started up the welfare debate in earnest during his 1992 presidential campaign when he called for "ending welfare as we know it." What he had in mind was a reform of the system that would help welfare recipients—mostly women with young children—to become self-supporting through paid work. After his election, his welfare experts, including Mary Jo Bane, began to draft a new law that would subsidize job training, day care, medical benefits, and supplemental transitional income to aid people on welfare as they moved into the job market. Initially, the new plan would cost more than simply passing out welfare checks. If it worked, however, the costs would presumably go down as the welfare rolls decreased.

But adamant opposition to the very idea of welfare had reached such a point by the mid-'90s that a plan increasing its costs could not even be considered—especially after the 1994 election put Congress in conservative Republican control. So the administration began the process of compromise that resulted, in 1996, in the abandonment of welfare entitlements and the resignation of Bane and Peter Edelman, as I've already mentioned.

What remains to be considered, in the context of a generally collapsing care system, is why opposition to welfare had grown so strong. And again, the starting place is the ideology of the private, applying here to the responsibility for family care.

The reigning idea is not at all complicated: the private family is responsible for family care and should provide for it through its own resources. The corollary idea is that the public should assume responsibility only when the family, due to circumstances beyond its control, cannot provide necessary care. But here is where the question does get complicated: What kinds of circumstances should the public regard as beyond the control of the private family? The short answer is not many, because basic confidence in private institutions—market and family—sets up the assumption that trouble anywhere in these systems is caused not by uncontrollable events but by wrongdoing. And the further assumption is that the right response of government in such cases is to rid the system of whatever is wrong.

When the first welfare programs began in the 1930s, the circumstances were a crippling national depression and families left destitute when the breadwinner, usually the husband and father, was unemployed, had deserted his family, or had died. These were widely accepted as emergency situations, unforeseen and unavoidable. But by the 1990s, many families in need were headed by women who were divorced or never married, and were unemployed because they had young children at home or because they lacked marketable skills.

To opponents of welfare, it looked as if these women were not victims of circumstance but creators of the circumstances in which they lived. Why had they not married? Why were they divorced? Why did they give birth to children they couldn't support? Why had they not developed marketable skills so that they could support themselves in the workforce without public help? In other words, unemployed single mothers were wrongdoers. They had brought trouble on themselves. Therefore, they were not entitled to public support.[3]

But this analysis rests on a huge fallacy masking the fact that the care problem extends far beyond women on welfare. The fallacy lies in the assumption that, in the rest of the society, families *can* provide good care for their members on the basis of their earnings. In fact, even with two adults working full-time, many families cannot meet all of their needs well. And the basic problem is not wrongdoing. It is, as we've seen earlier, the pressure of economic and social changes that have drawn most women out of the home and into the paid workplace. Without that enormous at-home, unpaid labor force, the system of private responsibility for family care breaks down—and breaks down most severely at low income levels. The math doesn't work. It cannot.

Here is the basic reality, sitting like an elephant in the living room, behind the ideology of private responsibility for family care: *Without women's full-time unpaid caretaking labor, families must buy needed care in the private market, and most do not have sufficient resources to buy enough of it. Therefore, the system as a whole is undercapitalized, and the unavoidable result, on the whole, is inadequate care.*

A survey of the private care market operating under these constraints demonstrates this dismaying situation.

First, child care. At present—in 1998—there are 10 million children under the age of five with working mothers, so the overall need for child care is enormous. About 44 percent of these children are cared for by relatives, about 30 percent are in day-care centers or nursery schools, about 15 percent in family day-care homes, and the rest in the care of nannies or neighbors or baby-sitters. And there are problems inherent in each arrangement.

At the high end, where families can pay whatever the market price may be for good-quality care, the main problem—the one Zoë Baird faced—is availability, especially for at-home care. By the late '90s, with the economy strong, many women turned from domestic work to other occupations, setting off bidding wars for nanny services in affluent areas. But even with wages rising to $600 a week and higher, often with health insurance and other benefits offered, the supply of at-home caretakers remained limited—largely because long hours and multiple responsibilities make the work difficult. In any case, this is a child-care option out of reach for most families.

An alternative for those that are merely well-off but not wealthy—especially young, overworked, but not yet highly paid professionals with young children—has been the au pair system. Organized by the United States Information Agency (USIA) as a cultural exchange program, a labor pool of young, generally well educated Europeans is imported to provide live-in child care for relatively low salaries—about $140 a week—plus the opportunity to take courses and to enjoy the experience of living and traveling in the United States.

The problem here is the difficulty of ensuring quality. The training that the program requires is minimal, and the potential duties are heavy. That is, the typical au pair—who may be as young as eighteen and is often and understandably more interested in social excitement than either education or child care—can be asked to spend up to forty-five hours a week, on her own, responding to the constant, exhausting needs and demands of infants and other children. And the consequences for the children may be harmful—or in some terrible cases, fatal.

A 1998 Massachusetts murder trial, televised in its entirety, brought all of the weaknesses of the au pair system into high relief. Louise Woodward, an eighteen-year-old from England who was living in the home of two young doctors to care for their two children—an eight-month-old baby and a toddler—was accused of killing the baby by violent shaking and a severe blow to the head. The claim was that the baby's fussy crying had driven her to a point of uncontrolled frustration. The defense was that the baby's crying and death were due to a prior head injury, the internal results of which had worsened to a fatal point. The jury, rejecting evidence of a prior injury, found Woodward guilty of second-degree murder. The judge, however, reduced the verdict to manslaughter, finding that Woodward had caused the baby's death by rough handling, but had not done so intentionally. In other words, he accepted the idea of frustration overwhelming the young woman's judgment and control.

The case received extraordinary attention nationwide as it provoked in all kinds of families a welter of anxieties about mothers working outside the home, about the safety of child care, about its availability and expense—in other words, about all of the conflicts created by the collapse of a care system that had not caught up to women's greatly changed place in the society. But as powerful a talisman of trouble as this case was, it resolved nothing. Both Massachusetts senators, Edward Kennedy and John Kerry, called for more stringent regulation of the au pair system, but USIA director Joseph Duffey said that similar efforts in the past had been defeated by the nonprofit agencies running the system and responding to the unremitting demand for affordable home help.

But "affordable" is a relative term. Au pairs, however modestly paid, are still too costly or too difficult to accommodate for most families. More accessible and more widely used are commercial day-care centers—although here, too, the expense of high-quality care limits its general availability.

Specifically, to achieve high quality, day-care centers must meet well-established operating standards: small groups of children, high staff-child ratios, well-educated and well-trained care providers, low provider turnover. And the costs of maintaining these standards, particularly the costs of salaries high enough to attract and keep well-trained staff, are beyond the financial capability of centers operating mainly on payments from families of ordinary means. Again, the math doesn't work—unless the centers receive subsidies from some source.

And that is exactly the problem. There are subsidies, but only for specific populations, not for the great majority of families.

For those at very low income levels, good quality day care may be available through charitable subsidies—largely in the form of church-based or volunteer-staffed centers, or through federal and state subsidies for families moving off welfare.

Higher up the income scale, employees of large corporations may have access to company-subsidized day-care centers as part of a benefit package, and such care is generally the best financed of all. But even here there is some cause for alarm.

The availability of corporate funding has spurred the growth of national for-profit day-care chains run by publicly traded companies. In April 1998, for example, Bright Horizons Inc. of Cambridge, Massachusetts, and Corporate Family Solutions Inc. of Nashville, Tennessee, announced a planned merger that would create a new company operating 255 preschool centers for 244 corporate clients in forty states. With the merger they anticipated expansion funded by increased investment. Seeing the same investment opportunity, Michael Milken, the former junk bond financier convicted of securities fraud, founded his own company—Knowledge Universe—and began to acquire employer-supported day-care centers and preschools already operating nationwide. The problem, of course, for companies answerable to investors, is the possible conflict of profitability and quality, even in well-financed places.

But in any case, corporate-financed care centers serve only a tiny percentage of the country's families. Many companies that do provide such service extend it to their regular employees only, excluding contingent or temporary workers, who make up an increasing percent-age of the workforce.[4] More common yet are companies that make some gesture toward their employees' caretaking needs, but by offering only marginal supports. They might contribute to the training of care workers to increase the local supply, support a day-care registry or emergency care hot line, provide start-up funds for new programs or equipment at local centers, and in rare cases, they might supplement care-provider salaries. They do not, as a rule, support operating ex-penses for centers on an ongoing basis. Then there are the great major-ity of firms, including virtually all small companies, that contribute little or nothing to day care.

Here, in the unsubsidized portion of the care market, is where most American families find themselves. And it is here that built-in eco-nomic pressure—the limited income of those buying care services—pushes the quality of day care downward.

Centers depending mainly on the resources of low- and middle-income families can offer only low wages to their care providers and therefore have great difficulty attracting and keeping well-qualified staff. In the late '90s, the nationwide starting salary for child-care teachers with college degrees was $15,000 to $16,000—and most such degree holders were choosing to enter school teaching at substan-tially higher salaries. Nonprofessional entry-level salaries rarely run much higher than minimum wage, particularly at national for-profit chains—which, in 1998, had begun to hire welfare recipients with few employment choices for their lowest-paying jobs.

The long-range effect of low wages is to keep the educational level of caregivers from rising, as there is little economic incentive for them to invest time and money in training. The chronic effect is a high turnover rate, about 30 percent a year on average nationwide—a classic recipe for poor quality. Of four hundred child-care centers tested in 1993 by university researchers in California, Colorado, Connecticut, and North Carolina, 76 percent were adequate or better in their health and safety provisions but were below standard in the support their staffs were able to provide for child development. And the strongest factor in intellectual and social development, according to a 1998 Families and Work Institute study, is high—that is, expensive—staff-child ratios.[5]

There is the math again: middle- and lower-income families lack sufficient resources to support high quality in day-care centers without corporate or governmental subsidies.

And this is not the whole story. At lower income levels many families without some form of care subsidy cannot afford even the less expensive day-care centers, and instead turn to family day care. This is service provided in private homes, usually by women who take care of a group of children for fees substantially lower than in commercial centers.

Theoretically, such home care is licensed and regulated, but in reality, requirements are generally minimal and oversight often nonexistent. New York state, for example, has two regulatory levels, neither stringent. Family care providers may be licensed, which requires checks of their premises and staff and an initial fifteen hours of training, or they may be registered, which requires merely a mail-in form and the same fifteen-hour training period. The license allows a higher number of children per provider. Both types are subject to unannounced inspection, but these are, in practice, few and far between.[6]

Regulations in other states vary but are becoming increasingly lenient due to the pressing need for affordable care, especially since the 1996 federal welfare law put more parents of small children in the workforce at low wages. And the problem, of course, is quality. Many care providers do excellent work, but many more do not. A 1994 study by the Families and Work Institute found only 9 percent of the home care arrangements they surveyed "good," as opposed to 56 percent that were "adequate" or merely "custodial," and 35 percent "poor" or "disadvantageous."[7]

Then there is the form of unregulated care that is most widely used, and that is care by relatives. This may be very good or very poor, depending on family circumstances, but is likely to involve constant juggling of tight schedules and considerable stress. One form of relative care that is highly problematic is the constant care of children being done by young girls in poor families with parents at work. Chronicling the daily lives of these girls, barely beyond childhood themselves, sociologist Lisa Dodson writes that they "shoulder the burdens of family care without money, without public support, and at the profound cost of their attention to their own development."[8] In other words, both the children being cared for and their too-young care providers are suffering the lack of adequate child care for low- and middle-income families in this country. And this is not even to mention the lack of after-school care for older children.

This, then, is the sum total of a child-care system that depends on the private resources of private families who must turn to the private market to replace the care formerly provided by a labor force of unpaid women at home. It is a system that is plainly not working well.

Elders, the ill, the disabled. The problem here is long-term care, and the question is this: How can families without women at home full-time provide long-term care for frail or disabled elders, for the mentally ill, or for any family member, adult or child, who suffers a permanent condition making the normal functions of daily life difficult or impossible?

The problems posed by mental illness are particularly hard. According to the National Institute of Mental Health, nearly 2 million people age eighteen or older are diagnosed with schizophrenia each year. And at any one time, about 15 million suffer from major depression or manic-depressive illness. And these illnesses place great strains on families. Most people have little knowledge of the major disorders, and the symptoms can be bewildering or frightening. Further, the stigma attached to any psychiatric trouble can prompt families to ignore or deny it. In any case, those who are ill often resist the efforts of families to help them. And in the era of deinstitutionalization—the replacement of long-term hospitalization by what is supposed to be community-based care—the availability of effective supports for the mentally ill is generally piecemeal, scattershot, and hard to negotiate.

Federal Social Security programs may provide health insurance and income supplements. State programs may provide food, housing, and supervised medication in group homes, as well as vocational education and job placement. Managed care companies may offer, in addition to diagnosis and medication, various ongoing services such as group support sessions, emergency hot lines, and family counseling. Advocacy organizations, notably the Alliance for the Mentally Ill, provide education and support for families dealing with mental illness. But identifying available programs, applying for benefits, locating effective vocational training, or knowing where to turn in an emergency can prove to be overwhelming hurdles—especially for people in a state of anxiety, panic, depression, or paranoia. And helping to find such services, where they exist, may be overwhelming as well for family members who must spend extraordinary amounts of time at this task—and may still fail.

The upshot is that without well-integrated, well-signposted, well-financed, and well-staffed community services for the mentally ill, only the most aggressive, persistent, and articulate among them—or those whose families have sufficient wealth or time and sophistication to help effectively—can make the care system work for them.

Then there is the problem of care for the elderly and others with chronic physical disability—that is, the problem of daily, continuing, long-term care for people who cannot, in some significant way, take care of themselves. Whose responsibility is this? As in the case of child care, the traditional answer places responsibility on the family, and specifically on the women of the family. But as is also true with child care, the women of the family—wives, daughters, granddaughters, and cousins—are no longer in their traditional places, available to provide the help that is needed. Yet we have constructed no other answer, except for the wealthy, who can finance their own long-term care, or for low-income elders, who can receive nursing-home care through Medicaid. For the middle class, once again, the dilemma is stark, and particularly so in the case of elders.

Two-thirds of the disabled elderly live at home or with relatives, which means that most long-term care is home care, and at low and middle incomes, support for such care is minimal. Medicare funds some medical procedures received at home, but mainly for acute rather than chronic conditions. And to keep costs down, particularly after cutbacks in the 1997 Balanced Budget Act, Medicare officials have imposed stringent limits on eligibility even for the home care they do support. Managed care plans also limit payments for home care, while at the same time limiting hospital stays so that patients return home still needing extensive care.

But what is most difficult for disabled elders and their families is to arrange needed help with the ordinary daily functions of eating, dressing, toileting, moving between bed to wheelchair, or with somewhat more complicated activities such as shopping, managing money, or

doing housework. This is often the kind of help that is essential to
allow people to stay in their homes, but there is little public funding
for it—in spite of the fact that it is far less expensive than nursing-
home care, which is generally the alternative. State programs may provide some support for nonmedical home services, but usually only for
low-income elders and for specific, limited tasks.

The result, of course, is that millions of families strain to take care of
relatives. In the mid-'90s an estimated 22.4 million households—
nearly one in four—were providing home care for family members or
friends over the age of fifty.[9] And usually such work entails great cost,
whether financial, physical, or emotional, to the person doing it.

Here is a story you could hear, with variations, in communities of all
kinds across the country. A young neighbor of mine in Cambridge left
a lucrative Silicon Valley job and returned to Massachusetts to help her
stroke-weakened but fiercely independent father continue living at
home—only to enter a nightmarish saga of limited, episodic support
for the elderly outside the nursing-home system.

Taking on most of the needed care herself, she found that her tasks
included doing three or four loads of laundry a day as her father became incontinent, arguing with him to submit to showers and diaper-
ing changes, pureeing his food when his dentures no longer fit and he
refused to get new ones, and waiting to let in various home caregivers—who, working at very low wages, often made their rounds on
city buses and could not predict their arrival times. She also spent
hours on the phone or in offices fending off efforts by the Visiting
Nurses Association to carry out Medicare cutbacks on chronically
needed care. Her father's eligibility to receive skin care for peripheral
vascular disease expired after one year, she was repeatedly told, even
though his vulnerability to skin lesions could not be prevented—as his
doctor attested.

At one low point a nursing supervisor warned the daughter that by
assuming responsibility for her father's home care, she became crimi-
nally liable for elder abuse if she did not provide twenty-four-hour supervision to guard against injury through falls or other mishaps.

Still, the father was able to stay at home until his last few weeks,
which he spent comfortably in a small, local hospice. The daughter,
however, was left physically and emotionally exhausted—and profes-

sionally derailed for several years as the irregular hours of needed care compromised her job opportunities.

And recall the story of the woman who could not bear to accept inferior nursing-home care for her dying mother, could not afford regular home nursing care, could not provide it herself without quitting her job, and ended up, with a bad conscience, employing an illegal alien nurse forced by her irregular status to work for lower-than-normal nursing wages.[10]

WHEN FAMILIES CANNOT PROVIDE the various kinds of care that their children or elders or others may need, and when public supports are not available because families are *supposed* to take care of themselves, the unmet need for care has to go somewhere. Generally it spills over onto public institutions that were not designed—and are not funded—to handle it. This is most marked in the case of children, with public schools taking up responsibilities, and costs, that families cannot sustain.

In a middle-class Massachusetts town, for example, a longtime teacher described the new responsibilities she assumes in the mid-'90s classroom. For one thing, she has thirty-four children in her third-grade class, with seventeen of them on Individual Education Plans designed to deal with learning problems. This startling ratio is not unusual,[11] and probably relates to the lack of time parents have to read with children and provide other cognitive stimulation at home. And beyond remedial work, and the basic third-grade subject matter, the veteran teacher says she must add instruction on handling problems specifically produced by the absence of adult supervision after school.

"We teach children how to deal with danger," she said, "what to do when they're at home alone—I don't remember having to teach that years ago. Now, we even have to teach them about computer and phone safety, because they can be reached that way. They have to learn more about nutrition because many of them are making their own choices about what to eat."[12]

After-school care is also a problem for the superintendent of schools in one of the wealthiest suburbs in the state, but for her it takes a strikingly different form. The educated, dual-career parents in this town demand extensive after-school programs and services. But teachers, pressed into late-afternoon and evening activities and meetings with anxious parents, protest that their own children are at home alone. And mothers who opt to stay at home, as well as residents without children in the schools, resent the rising costs of extra programs and mount angry taxpayer campaigns to cut school budgets. For these people, after-school care does not seem to be a legitimate public charge.

But the problems of poverty are, of course, the most dire. A school nurse in a poor Boston neighborhood conducts a weekly asthma club for children living in crowded, poorly ventilated, high-stress homes. On a normal morning, in addition to dealing with routine checkups, headaches, and stomach upsets, she gets a child to a hospital emergency room without calling an ambulance, which neither the child's family nor the school could pay for, calms a girl with an eye infection while finding a Spanish-speaking teacher to talk with the patient's mother at her job at Wendy's, and teaches a class on sexually transmitted diseases and sexual harassment. Here again the problem is to deal with unsupervised after-school hours—prime time for teenage sex, unplanned pregnancies, drug use, and violent crime. But valiant school nurses, whose basic function is to deal with illness, cannot make up the hours of care that neither families nor the market can provide.[13]

Then there is the issue of special education programs funded for disabled children but increasingly used for students with emotional and behavioral problems stemming not from actual disabilities but from social ills. In 1997, the *Boston Globe* reported a long list of cases culled from state records showing that "parents are using special education as a way to get services for children they don't have time for," and as a consequence, the schools "are being forced to drain money from regular education to pay for . . . students whose problems are not educational."[14]

The courts are similarly burdened. West Virginia state court judge Richard Neely, in *Tragedies of Our Own Making: How Private Choices Have Created Public Bankruptcy*,[15] has issued a broadside protest against the "explosion of demand to substitute government services for family." These services, he says, were meant to deal with extraordinary burdens that fall on a few people, such as care for a retarded child or unusually troubled adolescents, or extremities of poverty or abuse. But as it is now, he maintains, large portions of the population cannot provide adequate care for children, who then become the charges of social agencies and juvenile courts. And the costs of added social services eat up local budgets that must also support schools, police, and fire departments.

Neely is right, of course, that the present structure of government services, including the schools, was never meant to, and cannot as currently structured and funded, make up for the child care that private families no longer provide. But so far we are stuck trying to manipulate the old formulas in new ways to yield the needed care, and we are repeatedly coming up short.

So where do we turn next? Are women supposed to leave paid employment and return home to do care work again on the old terms? How can they if their families depend on the incomes of women as well as men? The median contribution to family income of married women working full-time is approaching 50 percent. And if the old division of labor were somehow restored, how could women pursue the promise of equality? Are they supposed to give it up?

The fact is—and it is an irreducible fact—the old formulas cannot yield both care and equality. They are bankrupt. And they are generating a social crisis that cannot be addressed realistically until we can remove the blinders of traditional thinking and take in the whole of what is happening.

But instead we find continued broad political backing for the idea that failures of the private systems—private market, private family—are due to wrongdoing, and that the solution should be a search for wrongdoers. Here, again, are the assumptions that lead to that search: caretaking is rightly a private responsibility; the private resources of the private family must support its need for care in all but exceptional circumstances; public responsibility is limited to aid in those exceptional circumstances; therefore, the role of government, beyond handling the exceptions, is to protect the integrity of the private family care system against wrongdoers undermining it.

We can hear this thinking articulated plainly in the words of an Ohio state representative discussing on *The Newshour with Jim Lehrer* the application in her state of the 1996 welfare reform law. The point of that law was precisely to assign to even the poorest families responsibility for their own care, with only minimal public support. Representative Joan Lawrence welcomed the reform and authored Ohio's plan for implementing it.

The question under discussion was what women who had lost their welfare benefits and were working at low-paying jobs could do about child care if day-care subsidies in the states were also terminated. One former welfare recipient in Ohio, a single mother who had just learned that she would soon lose a $300-per-month subsidy for child care, told an interviewer: "All I could think about was if it comes down to it, you know, I'm going to have to quit my job and take care of my child, stay at home and take care of my child . . . and go back on welfare."

But Representative Lawrence said, "She will not be able to go back on welfare . . . because [under the new regulations] you cannot quit a job unless you have good cause. And not having child care is not good cause for quitting a job, so just rule that out."

Then commenting further on efforts of advocates to reinstate the child-care subsidies, she added, "What would be the point of getting rid of the entitlement to welfare and then replace it with another entitlement that would grow and grow for child care? I don't think the public wants that. I certainly don't want it. What we're doing is teaching people, trying to help them become self-reliant, and use their own sense of responsibility to manage their family affairs."

Her solution is to create a larger pool of inexpensive care providers by easing government regulation of day care through "a registration system where your next-door neighbor can register to be reimbursed and just meet minimum safety and health standards." In other words, she would turn to a market solution that, as the studies previously mentioned have shown, would yield, for the most part, only low-quality child care for low-income parents.[16]

But from Representative Lawrence's point of view, the problems in the family care system follow from wrongdoing, and the wrongdoers are non-self-reliant mothers, the advocates of entitlements to publicly funded welfare and child care, and government itself, if it does provide such aid. The proper role of government is to enforce the natural efficiencies of the private systems, not to take over their functions.

Judge Neely casts a wider net, looking beyond the delinquencies of people in poverty to broader reasons for the breakdown of family responsibilities for care. The wrongdoers, in his view, are all those who put themselves in situations that undermine their ability to give adequate care to their children. This includes unwed mothers without the means to support their children, but also divorced parents who cannot or do not give sufficient time to their children, and parents who both "become so absorbed by outside work that parenting functions suffer." The wrong is that lack of sufficient care breeds trouble, with the result that "childrearing costs are externalized onto the rest of society." His solution is to restore social reliance on the two-parent family and to reinvigorate the idea that parents have a social duty to provide many hours of caregiving themselves or to pay for a high-quality alternative.[17]

But remember the math—it doesn't work. Constructing two-parent households would not, magically, put someone at home to do full-time caretaking. Wage structures would still make two incomes necessary for many families. Time demands in the workplace would still impose long hours on many parents. Family income may still not be enough to pay for all of the care that children and elders and others need. And, of course, math isn't the only problem. Even if one parent earned a family-supporting income, the other might still want to work in some way outside the home.

The next great task for American liberals, then, is to break through the limits imposed by old ideologies and to ask the key question: How can we organize good care for everyone who needs it, without constructing a class of caretakers excluded from the pursuit of equality?

This is a problem that calls for a redrawing of the boundary between private and public responsibility. It calls for a shifting of some responsibility for care to the society at large, some different allocation of caretaking costs, some new division of paid and unpaid labor. It calls for the adoption of care as a national political value.

CHAPTER 3

CARE AS A NATIONAL POLITICAL VALUE

THE FIRST PREMISE of a serious liberal politics of family care must be to recognize care as a national social value rightfully calling on Americans for meaningful support as a matter of high priority.

Such a move would be a leap for mainstream American liberals. Focused strongly on questions of economic injustice, liberal activists and politicians have never mounted a clear challenge to the long-prevailing assumption that, beyond poverty, care was strictly a family matter, a private responsibility.

The liberal stance on family issues, however, has not been so firm as that of conservatives. The ideology of the private, for conservatives, is an active principle, the purpose of which is to place control over private lives beyond the reach of governmental power. The private market, the private family—these are the two touchstones of conservative belief. Liberals, on the other hand—I've mentioned this earlier—have recognized and responded to several problems in this tradition. One is that oppressive outside pressures can come not just from government but from the market, which chronically puts many families below a decent level of self-support. Another is that the practice of dividing labor by sex—male breadwinner/female caretaker—generally restricts women's control over their own lives. It is a practice, therefore, that re-

stricts for them the quintessential liberal principles of individual freedom and equality.

But suspicion of the private systems has not moved liberals to think
about families and their caretaking function as a clear-cut matter of
public concern, partly because they, too, are wary of government intrusion into private spaces. And partly they have been wary of the family
itself, as an institution, precisely because its traditional operation sometimes subjected its members—particularly women and children—to
claims that could crowd individual rights.

The consequence has been some openness in liberal politics to problems of family care but still no clear recognition of the care crisis, as
such. Rather, as the now familiar troubles began to edge into public
view—concerns about day-care costs, maternity leaves, latchkey children, untended elders—liberals tended to think about such matters as
"women's issues." Thus, politically, women became a "special interest"
in the liberal camp, joining other special interests on a list of constituencies whose needs had to be taken into account—or resisted, depending on the pressures of the moment. Recall the newly elected Bill
Clinton's angry reaction to the "bean counters" who wanted yet more
women in the cabinet than the increased number he proposed. At that
point he was being accused of going too far to please liberal interests,
including women.

Necessarily lost in the conception of care as a women's issue, and of
women as a special interest, is the big picture—the country's care system collapsing and the conflict between care and equality adding its
pressure to the collapse.

However, this state of affairs is not static. In a book published just as
Bill Clinton was appearing on the national scene in 1991, psychologist
Arlene Skolnick announced that the conservative ownership of the
family issue was beginning to change. The change agents, she said,
were women caught in work-family pressures that led them to call for
public attention to such needs as prenatal care, day care, and parental
leave. "It seemed inevitable," she wrote presciently, "that a new politics
would sooner or later emerge to address the predicaments besetting the
family and the country, but there was no telling when the inevitable
would happen."[1]

I would argue that signs of a new family politics began to emerge in the presidential election campaign of 1996 when the Democratic Leadership Council found itself confronted by an unfamiliar and deeply perplexing question: Should Democrats base themselves, and their public appeal, on economic issues *or* on the problem of values?

The presidential advisers who had foregrounded economic security as the winning issue in Bill Clinton's 1992 campaign—James Carville and Stanley Greenberg—insisted that economics was still what mattered to people. And they were strongly seconded by such activists as Jeff Faux, president of the Economic Policy Institute, and advocacy journalist Richard Parker, who argued that the real and constant business of liberals was to secure the interests of the middle class in high wages, corporate responsibility for job security, and the just distribution of wealth from the top to the bottom of the income scale.[2]

But Bill Clinton's newly trusted pollster and strategist Dick Morris pushed a different message. The primary issue for the time, Morris insisted, was the great anxiety people were feeling about families, children, schools, drugs, and violence—worries about the basic "values" of American life.[3]

The values strategy was warmly defended by columnist E. J. Dionne Jr. against critics who found that concerns about flextime and parental leave and other work-family issues lacked the seriousness of "grand economic theories." Problems created by vast changes in the old division of labor, Dionne said, are deeply serious in their effects on the whole society.[4]

But another prominent liberal writer, Thomas Byrne Edsall, argued vociferously against the values approach as an appeal directed mainly at women. This was a mistake, he said, because it was precisely Bill Clinton's attention in his first two years to the special interests—women, along with gays, blacks, and other minorities—that undermined his support in the middle class and stymied any possibility of advancing an economic agenda that might best have benefited all such groups.[5]

Yet other liberals attacked Clinton for not taking values seriously enough. This message was most coherently pressed by Christian groups—Protestant and Catholic—that had formed the Call to Renewal, an umbrella organization intended to express the moral concerns of the left. The main themes of a national meeting in September 1996 were compassion for the poor, revived welfare programs, and acceptance and support for troubled, ostracized minorities.[6]

Bill Clinton—much to the chagrin of Republicans who accused him of stealing their ideas, and of Democrats who accused him of selling out on economic issues—listened to Dick Morris and began to talk insistently about the family.

His basic messages *were* directed at women, and women's concerns about the needs of families: education for children, Medicare for the elderly, police on the streets and an assault weapons ban for public safety, tax breaks for college students, environmental protections for health, the Family and Medical Leave Act for the work-family squeeze. He pointed to the administration's Violence Against Women Act, new child-support laws cracking down on deadbeat dads, proposed legislation prohibiting twenty-four-hour limits on hospital stays for childbirth, and, noting that his mother had died of breast cancer, his allocation of funds for breast cancer research. He also hailed the V-chip, school uniforms, neighborhood curfews, and campaigns against teenage smoking. And he won the election on the women's vote. Among men, he lost to Dole, although barely—44 percent to 43 percent. But women voted 54 percent to 38 percent for Clinton—a 16 percent gender gap.

Clinton's family focus in the 1996 election was, without question, poll-driven, the messages carefully calibrated by the omniverous opinion gatherer, Morris. And Clinton, as he had been throughout his presidency, was severely criticized for relying on polls rather than his own thought and conviction as a basis for policy. But public polling can be a measure of reality, and Morris's measurements did accurately reveal widespread distress about the state of the family. Clinton was, therefore—not in spite of his opportunistic poll reading but because of it—addressing real "predicaments besetting the family and the country."

This was a significant juncture in American politics. By making real family predicaments the central issue of a presidential campaign, Clinton had positioned the functioning of families as a public concern—and as a subject of liberal politics.

He had not, however, gone to the heart of the matter, nor had his liberal critics as they called either for a single focus on middle-class insecurities or for greater compassion for the poor. The critics, while rightly focusing on economic need, were not grasping the significance of the family-care crisis. Clinton, honing in with great exactitude on the family, was dealing with economic issues in a separate category. Minimum wage. Investment in education. Economic strength through balanced budgets, increased exports, and so forth. That is, the Clinton family policy consisted of a generally strong economy plus a scattering of specific family aids.

But a serious politics of family care must go beyond such a formula. It must explicitly link economics and the function of caretaking. It must begin with a clear view of the unfair allocation to women of the major costs of caretaking, as reviewed in chapter 1, and clear recognition of critical deficits in the present care system, as reviewed in chapter 2. And then, with the whole picture of these systemic costs and deficits firmly in mind, the liberal community must work on the invention of a new care system.

This is a project requiring a constant double focus. One object of attention must be the ideas, the belief systems, and particularly the ideology defining proper private and public functions that justify present care practices and keep them in place. Liberals have to formulate and conduct a public discussion about a different set of ideas and values and priorities, a positive social responsibility for care. Then the second part of the project is to design new policies. But I cannot emphasize enough the importance of supplying a positive new way of thinking about care as a public issue, because without new concepts in place, the old idea barriers will inevitably block whatever specific policies liberals propose.[7]

THE KEY IDEA for a new politics of family care, as I've said at the outset, is to add care to the pantheon of national social values. That is, to assure good care to all members of the society should become a primary principle of our common life, along with the assurance of liberty, equality, and justice.

We need to elevate care to this level of importance for the basic reason that it is essential to human health and balanced development. It is also crucial to developing human moral potential, to instilling and reinforcing in an individual a sense of positive connection to others. And it is this sense of connection that makes possible the whole range of mutual responsibilities that allow the people of a society to respect and work toward common goals. As political theorist Joan Tronto puts it, thinking about care seriously, recognizing that everyone at different times is both a giver and a receiver of care, underscores for people the *fact* of their personal and social interdependence. And, she says, this insight can enhance a commitment to the responsibilities of democratic citizenship.[8]

Starting with the value of care as a national priority, liberals need next to break away from the idea that care in that context consists only of ministering to people who for some reason—age, illness, disaster, poverty—are helpless and cannot take care of themselves. A liberal conception of care would include all of the thought and work that organizes all of the caring that supports everyone's everyday life.

Six-month-old babies obviously need attentive care, but so do sixteen-year-old high schoolers. They need to be listened to. They need the kind of guidance that can take a parent hours to think through carefully before saying a word. Families need time for adults to read to children and to talk with each other about the day. They need time for the inevitable emergencies—from strep throat to heart attack to depression to broken hips. And they need time for the dailiness of laundry, shopping, cleaning—and eating.

That sharing food is a central element of family life, that it is highly important to creating and sustaining social bonds in any group, is well understood. But sociologist Marjorie DeVault explores the significance of what is generally not seen, and that is the actual work involved in buying, cooking, and serving food—the time, the skill, and "the effort of being constantly responsive and attentive" that precedes the moment when food arrives at the table. She calls this whole effort "sociability work." It is work that keeps people nourished, not only physically but emotionally and psychically, as it constantly reinforces relations of intimacy and connection. It is work, DeVault insists, that is essential to a society operating on principles of basic respect for others.[9] In other words, a system that valued care would be organized to allow time for sociability work—and for the whole range of family activities that support well-being.

A further essential idea is that the need for socially supported care, broadly understood, runs across all income levels. And this is an idea that liberals especially need to confront, as they have tended to focus heavily on the family problems of the poor. Of course, the poor do need particular attention, but liberals need to widen the context of their concern, because by focusing on poverty as a special circumstance, they leave untouched the idea of family care as solely a private responsibility. Implicitly they ratify the assumption that all is well for everyone else, that all other families can take care of themelves out of their own resources. And in doing so they create problems across the board.

One is the difficulty of defending against conservative arguments that the poor, too, could take of themselves, if they tried hard enough—a winning argument in the welfare debate, and one enshrined in the title of the 1996 antiwelfare law, the Personal Responsibility and Work Opportunity Act.

But the further problem is even more serious if less immediately obvious. To act as if only the poor need protection leaves families in all income brackets dealing with market forces generally blind to family needs. Whether the market demands too much time from workers, or returns too little money, or both, caretaking suffers throughout the society, not just below the poverty line. The liberal vision has to extend to the whole picture, the whole system.

To see the whole and describe it politically, liberals need to adopt one more general idea as a basis for a policy portfolio, and that is the idea of constructing a national accounting system for caretaking. Care is work. It costs something. And we have to think about how much we need and who should pay the costs.

And here is where the significance of the traditional unpaid care labor force looms large. We have been able not to think politically about the costs of our caretaking system as a whole because, with women at home, care seemed costless—even though it exacted the great social cost of excluding women from full and equal participation in the affairs of the society. In any case, we still literally do not count, in the gross domestic product, the "production" of care that is unpaid.

This has not always been the case. According to economist Nancy Folbre, various official accounts of economic activity used to categorize domestic work as productive—meaning a contribution to national wealth. But around the middle of the nineteenth century, as the industrial revolution took hold, the designation changed. At first, new methods of accounting listed housewives separately, then as "unoccupied," then as "dependents," and finally simply left them out. Officially, the women at home disappeared from public sight, along with the domestic work they continued to do.[10]

Now we do include paid care in the GDP, but we do not have clear sight of the unpaid care work being done, nor, significantly, the needed care work *not* being done. And while we know from various studies and from common experience that women still do most of the country's home care, we do not have a clear common understanding of how much work that is, nor of what doing it means for the women caregivers—positively and negatively. We need a running accounting so that we know how much care we have, how much care we need, what its costs are now, particularly for women, and what the costs would be for a better, fairer system.

THIS IS WHERE THE DESIGN of policy comes in. A liberal design, recognizing care as a national value and defining its meaning broadly, would ask for contributions to good care from everyone in some way—through responsibility in workplaces, in government, and in families.

Of the three, the most important for change in the country's care system is the workplace, because it is hours of work and wage levels that have the most direct effect on the way families can organize their lives. And for many people, women especially, it is the tyranny of time at work—long or inconvenient or unpredictable hours—that most severely compromises their ability to provide a reasonable amount of care for various family members.

Take the case of Joanna Upton—literally a court case decided by the Massachusetts Supreme Judicial Court in 1997. Upton, the single mother of a young son, sued her former employer for wrongful dismissal from her job when she was fired for refusing to work overtime—until nine or ten at night—because of family responsibilities. She had been told when she was hired that her hours would be 8:15 to 5:30, but she found that her duties as a manager kept her at work until six or seven every evening even before the overtime was demanded.

The firing, she claimed, was illegal as a violation of Massachusetts public policy favoring the care and protection of children. But the court dismissed her claim on the grounds that an at-will employee may be fired "for any reason or for no reason at all" unless the firing violates a "clearly established" public policy. And it concluded that Massachusetts had "no public policy which mandates that an employer must adjust its expectation, based on a case-by-case analysis of an at-will employee's domestic circumstances. . . ."[11]

There is the care-equality-time problem in a nutshell. Even without "overtime," Upton was working ten-hour days, and with commuting time added in, scarcely seeing her son. Her choice was to accept that situation or suffer a career setback because there was no public policy system that made any of that relevant to her employer. The question is *how* to make it relevant, *how* to construct public policy that makes family time part of an employer's concern.

One approach being developed by management theorists is to demonstrate that employers as well as employees can benefit from work hours that support both family care and women's equal opportunity at work.

Advanced most notably by Professor Lotte Bailyn of MIT's Sloan School of Management, the basic idea is that various types of work systems can be made compatible with family needs for time at home *and* women's needs for equal opportunity at work without losses—and sometimes with gains—in productivity and profit.

Bailyn starts from the premise that efforts to reduce the work-family squeeze by relying on policies now regarded as "family-friendly"— maternity leave, emergency day care, on-site regular day care, flextime, part-time—are actually hardening the lines of inequality for women.

The essential problem, she says, lies in deeply rooted assumptions about the nature of work and the workplace. One is the idea that the business world is a separate place with separate concerns from the private domestic domain, and has no responsibility for it. This is exactly the idea reflected by the Massachusetts Supreme Judicial Court in the *Upton* case. The other assumption is that the most valuable employee puts work first, and commitment to work first is measurable in terms of time, of long hours committed to the job.

These assumptions compel most workers to fit in time with families in pressured segments, sometimes a matter of minutes at the beginning and end of a day, sometimes not that. This is a state of affairs that sociologist Arlie Hochschild says actually induces many people to put in extra time at work because the piled-up problems at home are painful to face when there is too little time to deal with them.[12] And those workers—mostly women—who do not accept the prevailing workplace ethic and instead opt for flextime or part-time or family leave, demonstrate that they are not committed to work first. Therefore, they are unlikely to be valued highly and promoted, and gender inequity stays in place.

So, Bailyn argues, the family-friendly approach, superimposed on the existing assumptions shaping the workplace, is not the way to go. Rather, any movement toward family support and equal opportunity for women has to focus on changing the assumptions—and then to promote restructured hours and work assignments consciously designed to honor family time. Such a system operating generally and applicable to everyone should have the particular benefit to women of protection against being stigmatized or penalized for giving time to families.

And the benefit to employers should be a workforce with less tension, less fatigue, better focus, less absenteeism, lower turnover, higher morale generally—and the talents of women who might otherwise quit or remain in part-time, lower-level jobs where their abilities would not be fully expressed.

Conducting pilot programs with teams of advisers in divisions of three major corporations—Xerox, Corning, and Tandem Computers—Bailyn demonstrated that the restructuring she advocated was indeed possible. In several instances, for example, managers tried structuring the work of their departments in teams, as opposed to separate divisions, to allow a broadly flexible shifting of functions. And this, they found, produced both increased efficiency and the possibility for workers to stagger work hours as best suited family needs. And a later project carried out with Fleet Financial Services clearly documented increased levels of worker satisfaction along with sustained or increased productivity.

But, as Bailyn and her colleagues found, moving from one work system to another presents inevitable difficulties. Extensive group discussions between the advisory teams and company administrators were needed in several sites to convince managers even to look at work-family concerns and productivity issues in relation to each other. For example, managers on a production line would typically assume that work problems, such as complaints about the quality of a product, were their responsibility alone. That is, they would assume that in solving the problem, perhaps by imposing longer hours and more controls on the workforce, they did not have to take into account the effect of such changes on workers' family lives. In fact, it would usually not occur to them to do so; workers' personal problems—or "domestic circumstances" as the Massachusetts court put it—were the business of the human resources department.

It proved possible for the Bailyn teams to alter this mode of thought, but it took considerable time. And then there was a further problem with keeping new practices in place. With inevitable shifts in personnel, incoming managers who had not gotten the news of the new approach would revert to the old assumptions. In other words, when a company culture divided work and family as separate spheres—which most do—that conception would assert itself almost automatically unless there was constant pressure against it.[13]

Also, there are instances, although the Bailyn projects did not deal with this, when reorganizing work for the benefit of families cannot be costless to the employer, when it would necessarily be a matter of shifting some of the costs of care out of families and into the corporate world—essentially returning a greater share of corporate income to workers, less to managers and stockholders.

Measures for accomplishing this result would include higher corporate contributions to day care and other family-care arrangements—although the problem here is to be sure that such corporate policies are not designs to underwrite increased work hours. One mechanism intended to protect both time and income for employees is work-shift analyst Ronald Healey's 30/40 plan—a workweek compressed to thirty hours but paid at a forty-hour rate. *U.S. News and World Report's* 1998 guide to the best jobs found the 30/40 plan operating in some manufacturing companies and increasingly in the health care industry.

But there are obvious limits to the ability of workers, even that small percentage effectively backed by unions, to gain a satisfactory balance of income and work hours from employers. And it is here that responsibility for promoting the twin goals of care and equality falls to government. It is here also that liberals need to foster vigorous public discussion to legitimate the involvement of government in work-family issues.

Bill Clinton made at least a gesture toward such a discussion as part of the family focus of his 1996 campaign. In May 1996, the White House sponsored a Corporate Citizenship Conference, the purpose of which was to focus on the need for companies to take active responsibility for conditions that affect their employees' lives, and to honor specific corporate leaders who were doing so. Citing flexible work hours, on-site child care, and paternity leave among other work policies, Clinton insisted that there was now ample proof that "you can do the right thing and make money."[14]

This was, of course, a message that did not confront the hard issues. The president did not speak about the need for the business world to assume responsibility for work-family solutions with costs attached. And he did not introduce the complication of women's equality as part of the total picture. But his adoption of the term "corporate citizenship" was significant. Citizenship is a political term. To call a corporation a citizen is to acknowledge that it is a political entity, part of a polity made up of other citizens. It is to acknowledge that corporations have social responsibilities, and not just when those responsibilities are cost-free. This is terminology that liberals should make their own in pressing a governmental agenda.

What, then, should the agenda be?

On the issue of releasing workers' time for home care, there is a clear need to extend the Family and Medical Leave Act—which, as I've said earlier, was no more than a tiny gesture when adopted in 1993. Since then, several states have extended the federal law slightly. In May 1998, Massachusetts adopted the Small Necessities Leave Act, which requires companies with fifty or more employees to allow twenty-four hours of unpaid leave time a year to deal with such exigencies as visiting a child's school or accompanying a family member to a medical appointment. But larger steps are necessary.

Leaves need to be paid, at least in part, for most people to be able to use them. And the costs of paid leave, at least for small business, need to be spread through some kind of insurance or subsidy.

That such a system is by no means a pipe dream, beyond all bounds of possibility, is clear—I would say shamefully clear—from the various models of paid leave operating in all other economically advanced countries. European practice runs from the basic—Switzerland's ten weeks of leave with wage replacement at a flat rate—to the highly generous—Sweden's 72-week leaves at 90 percent of the leave-taker's pay. Some systems run on the country's all-purpose Social Security program, funded by contributions from employers and employees. Others are financed by general tax revenues, or some combination of taxes, Social Security, and employer or employee insurance funds.

According to economist Kirsten Wever, the key to the workability of these systems is the governmentally mandated application of paid leave policies to all companies so that none suffers a competitive disadvantage. And the costs to the economy as a whole are apparently offset by the creation of a labor pool widened by women willing to work if they are able to take leaves for family needs, and by reduced employee turnover.[15]

In short, the bar to paid leaves in the United States is not economic. It is ideological. It is the remaining mistaken belief in the beneficence of market forces, their ability to support the society's values blindly, automatically—which, of course, they cannot do.

A further form of governmental support for family care at home is a tax credit for the caregiver's work, an idea advanced by President Clinton in his 1999 State of the Union Address.

A tax credit, however, would be useful only to families in which one member earned a taxable salary. For low-income families, especially poor single-parent families, at-home care requires direct subsidy—that is, welfare in some form—and liberals should continue to insist on the value of supporting such care, at least for preschool children. Certainly they should continue to insist that moving welfare recipients into the workforce rarely provides sufficient income for decent family care.[16]

But support for good care need not take the form of replaying the welfare fight. More interesting and ultimately more beneficial are proposals being made by social theorists who would abandon the mechanism of welfare for direct income supports—in effect, a guaranteed annual income. One, unexpectedly enough, is the conservative economist Edmund Phelps; another, the liberal political scientist John Schwarz. Both suggest a form of across-the-board subsidies for low-wage workers to bring their incomes up to a level capable of decent support for a family.

As Phelps puts it, "The wage that private employers can afford to pay an employee is only the worker's *private* productivity," but "society has an interest in seeing work and other contributions rewarded according to their *social* productivity." And by social productivity he means "external benefits for the rest of the citizenry from one's ability to support oneself and to exercise responsibility as a citizen, community member, parent, and spouse." He envisions joint corporate-governmental contributions toward the needed subsidies, and argues strongly that the pathologies produced by poverty cost the country more than the subsidies would. Here is math that does work and that liberals should adopt as their own.[17]

Then, beyond poverty, and beyond at-home care for children, there is need for governmental support for various forms of paid care that low- and middle-income families cannot provide on their own, as discussed in the last chapter. Liberals have promoted many such programs for years—although with too little attention to middle-class needs.

For children, the familiar list includes support for high-quality paid day care and tax credits for families using it, support for early childhood care and education, and strong support for after-school programs. Thorough training for child-care providers and salary levels compensating for the valuable work they do require subsidy—probably in some combination of loans, scholarships, and grants. And regulations setting higher standards of training for au pairs and family-care providers are clearly needed, as is enforcement of training and safety standards in all forms of paid care. Most of the list was included in

President Clinton's child-care initiative proposed in January 1998 for his 1999 budget—although at levels of funding more modest than the actual need.

As in the case of family leave, the operating models for generous public support for child care are in Europe, where most countries provide automatic child allowances for all families at all income levels. Several subsidize child care from infancy to age three and offer free full-day preschools for three- to five-year-olds, as well as providing universal health care and housing allowances. Again, the resistance to such programs in the United States, which unquestionably has the wealth to support them, is ideological. And again, it is at the level of ideology that liberals must focus their first efforts.

For adults, including elders, the physically disabled, and the mentally ill, the major need, as we've seen, is support for long-term care in the home and community, and particularly for forms of support that go beyond medical needs.

The mentally ill and their families would benefit greatly from well-staffed community centers providing a comprehensive array of services in one place. But systemically, what is urgently needed is the extension of health insurance to cover mental illness adequately, more protected housing for those who cannot live on their own, wider availability of day hospitals for people in need of monitoring and intensive counseling for certain periods of time, and continued research to refine medications capable of relieving the torments of major mental illness with minimal side effects.

As for long-term elder care, clearly the greatest need is support for nonmedical home services. One positive trend is the development of various programs authorized to pool Medicare and Medicaid funding for the precise purpose of providing long-term, including nonmedical, home care for the frail elderly. But these are still essentially plans for those whose low income and asset levels qualify them for Medicaid. Others may be eligible to join the plans but at a substantial monthly fee. In other words, long-term care for the middle-income elderly remains largely unsupported.

Extending public support for long-term care to the middle class would, of course, mean greatly increased governmental funding and would depend on widespread acceptance of such care as, in part, a social responsibility. As with the other social programs discussed, gaining that acceptance against the assumption of sole private responsibility is the first—and difficult—liberal task.

To this point, I've been arguing that the work and the costs of care previously shouldered by families, and mainly by women in families, need to be more widely distributed throughout the society, with business and government assuming new levels of engagement. But for the country to construct new systems of care on terms of equality for women, caring work also needs to be redistributed within the family. And in most families this means it needs to be shared by women and men.

Studies differ as to whether signficant change in the division of family work is actually taking place. A 1998 Families and Work Institute survey of working mothers and fathers found marked increases in the amounts of time spent by men in both child and elder care. But social psychologist Carin Rubenstein declared the study flawed by "notoriously inaccurate" self-reported estimates of the times in question. She said that other studies based on more accurate daily logs report little change in the last thirty years, with mothers still outspending fathers on time with children by about four to one.[18]

As to what should be happening, the definitive liberal text is still Susan Moller Okin's *Justice, Gender, and the Family*. Here is her vision of what families would look like in a just future when equality had become a normal part of life.

> No assumptions would be made about "male" and "female" roles; childbearing would be so conceptually separated from child rearing and other family responsibilities that it would be a cause for surprise, and no little concern, if men and women were not equally responsible for domestic life or if children were to spend much more time with one parent than the other. It would be a future in which men and women participated in more or less equal numbers in every sphere of life, from infant care to different kinds of paid work to high-level politics. Thus it would no longer be the case that having no experience of raising children would be the practical prerequisite for attaining positions of the greatest social influence.[19]

Okin is making a crucial point. If responsibility for home care remained unequal, other reforms—restructured work hours, subsidized

child and elder care, and the rest—would not significantly change
women's position in the society. And this is true because good family
care takes time. That is the point of releasing and supporting time to
do it. Therefore, if women still did the bulk of it, they would still be
compromising their engagement in outside work and in public life.
Their voices in the activities and decisions that shape the way the society works would still remain limited. They would still remain unequal.

In short, the family is the third and vital part of what must be an
integrated and dynamic new system linking business, government,
and family if we are to replace old patterns with good care and real
equality.

BUT HERE WE RUN into another problem for liberals in the pursuit of
these ambitious goals. The liberal commitment to expanding the
bounds of public responsibility for the general welfare is well established. The liberal commitment to equality is firm, if somewhat under-
developed with respect to women. The liberal concern for care is
definite, if too narrowly framed historically as a problem of poverty.
But liberals, always strongly focused on the individual, on individual
rights and liberties and opportunities, have never made the family, as
an institution, their subject. This is a blank spot in the liberal tradition
that the next several chapters seek to fill.

PART TWO

EMBRACING
THE FAMILY

CHAPTER 4

MORAL PANIC: SEX, FAMILIES, POLITICS

FAMILIES ARE THE MAINSTAY of the American caretaking system. They always have been. They still are. And they should remain the primary source of care—with strong, clear, principled liberal support. But if mainstream liberals have difficulty reaching a clear-cut position on care as a broadly conceived, cross-class national value, they have even more trouble finding firm ground on the subject of families.

As we've seen, what liberals have done in the face of a spreading care crisis is to seek various economic supports, such as subsidized day care and health care, for hard-pressed families. But while such programs, where they operate, relieve serious stresses on the family, they cannot fill the cracks in family structures caused by radical shifts in the caretaking role of women. They do not speak to the nature of the family as such—what it is, what makes it a vital social unit, what, besides economic security, enables it to function well.

The underlying problem that all Americans face, of course, is that the family, as a social institution, has been battered over the last generation by a hurricane of change.

Long tradition had based the family on the heterosexual couple, married, faithful, in a permanent union. It assigned the familiar division of labor—women as caretakers, men as breadwinners. It set up lines of authority with the man of the family in charge. Tradition also defined sex roles. Men were entitled to sexual conquest and held the dominant position as initiators and controllers of sexual relations. Women's role was to beguile and seduce, but generally to follow the male lead. Sexual relations were to occur only within marriages. If pre-marital sex produced a pregnancy, the couple were to marry before the child was born. After marriage, a double standard allowed men extra-marital affairs but placed severe social—and legal—penalties on women who engaged in them. Women were to hold the family to-gether and to take care of its members. All of the traditional rules taken together supported the security and stability of the family and pro-tected its reproductive and caretaking functions.

But in the 1960s and 1970s, the rules began to crack. In addition to a restructuring economy, which pulled millions of women away from their home labor into the paid workforce, and the women's movement, which championed a world of new choices, a sexual revolution rewrote all the rules of marriage. And the consequences were stunning: the so-cial acceptance of sex outside of marriage; a license for teenage sex complete with advice columns for its conduct; women taking on the role of initiator in the sexual dance; gays and lesbians coming out of the closet; unmarried, including same-sex, couples living together; no-fault, socially accepted divorce; legally protected abortion; unmarried women having children, not just as a result of poverty or ignorance, but by choice, and—in the new social role of single parent—keeping and raising them.

The new principle running through this process of change is choice, individual choice in the shaping of intimate relations and family com-mitments. And choice, whether enacted through nonmarital sex, abor-tion, divorce, or gay relationships, necessarily runs counter to the code of prescribed obligations that historically held families together.

Couples have become far more accustomed than in the past to set their own terms for marriage and to leave if their expectations are not met. Lines of responsibility for children and other dependents have be-come diffuse through divorce and remarriage. More generally, the new pleasure-seeking mandate of a sexually emancipated society has under-mined to some degree the old, stern ethic of responsibility for the wel-fare of others.

This loss of family stability poses problems, but there were serious losses also under the old rules, especially for women. Not only did the traditional family system restrain personal behavior, it also effectively limited women's education, their engagement in other-than-family work, their employability in many workplaces, including the professions, their participation in public life, and their political voice. And the same rules denied the acceptability of gay relations altogether, thus permitting all kinds of discrimination against homosexuals.

Making these inequalities clear to the public and advocating change that widened individual choice in relation to families fell logically to liberals, whose political mission has always been to promote the liberty and equality of disadvantaged groups. But while resolutely promoting the cause of individual rights, liberals have not found a way of theorizing and emphasizing the importance of stable families at the same time.

What this has meant politically is that conservatives have owned the family issue. Moreover, they have succeeded in keeping the word "family" defined in traditional terms. And for many conservatives, including the most politically vocal and active, the tradition that defines families derives from a powerful moral imperative—nothing less than the law of nature, or of God.

In this view, nature has fitted men and women together through natural heterosexual desire and anatomy to produce children. Women's nurturant nature has fitted them to take care of the children and others. Men are by nature the dominators and protectors, and as the stronger sex, have a natural duty to remain in their marriages and provide for their families.

The ultimate authority on the nature of family for the many conservatives who are Christian fundamentalists is, of course, the Bible. Genesis 2:18–24 describes the union of man and woman as the basis for the human family with the creation of Eve from Adam's rib to be his partner. "That is why a man leaves his father and mother, and is united to his wife, and the two become one flesh." Leviticus 20:9–13 provides rules for the sanctity of marriage including condemnation of both adultery and homosexual acts. "If a man commits adultery with his neighbor's wife, both adulterer and adulteress shall be put to death." And "If a man has intercourse with a man as with a woman, they both commit an abomination. They shall be put to death; their blood shall be on their own heads."[1]

The significance of these beliefs is that the family roles and relations that follow from them, being natural, are immutable. People cannot simply decide to change what a family is. It has been designed by a power higher than the reach of human choice. Therefore, when people defy the traditional rules defining families, they are flying in the face of nature. They are defying the will of God. They are doing wrong. And their wrongdoing will inevitably produce harm, for themselves and the whole society.

Political debate about families, then, becomes an argument with fixed sides: Nature versus Choice. *Either* you stand for families *or* individual rights. And the intensity of conviction of both liberals and conservatives is so great that when particular issues arise—about abortion, for example, or homosexuality—the air is filled with anger and vituperation. Conservatives charge liberals with gross immorality. Liberals charge conservatives with sheer prejudice, misogyny, and homophobia.[2]

The problem in this shouting match for liberals is that conservatives are right in some of their claims of harm produced by the breakdown of old rules and weakened families. But because liberals reject conservative conceptions of the family, they have not paid enough attention to family issues as such. They have not thought enough about positive links between families and social health. They have not explicitly contested conservative conceptions of family by putting together the values of family and choice, family and rights.[3]

As a result, liberal policies dealing, for example, with poor single mothers and their children are not wholly coherent. They focus on clear, describable trouble, such as children without adequate food or care. But they are not squarely based on long-term, comprehensive programs for the sustenance of strong families—however family structures might be defined. And in the short term such policies—not strongly affirming what is valuable in families—are constantly vulnerable to conservative attack.

Bill Clinton hit this minefield in the early months of his tenure with yet another controversial choice for his administrative team—that of

Dr. Joycelyn Elders as surgeon general. Unlike Zoë Baird, Elders survived the confirmation process but, like Baird, soon fell victim to the political maelstrom surrounding families. Blunt and outspoken, she would last in office only fifteen months.

These were fifteen months, however, to which liberals need to pay close attention, because the battles that Elders fought, and lost, set out markers locating the liberal blind spot on matters of sexual morality, the place where new pro-family theory is needed to support the positions that she was trying—loudly and vividly—to move into national policy.

Joycelyn Elders as surgeon general, standing before the country in the uniform of a three-star admiral, presented a mind-bending picture. A black woman admiral. A sharecropper's daughter with a three-star badge of authority to oversee the nation's health. And there was a deeper dissonance as well.

The admiral's uniform, a carryover from the origins of the surgeon general's office in the Marine Hospital Service, denoted a warrior's approach to public health, a mission to fight disease as an enemy to be defeated. This, indeed, had been the usual operating mode of the Public Health Service, which succeeded the Marine Hospital Service and which the modern surgeon general headed. Spearheaded by a uniformed Commissioned Corps of physicians and technicians, it had, over the years, waged campaigns against bacteria in public water supplies, tobacco toxins that attack lungs and hearts, and contagions spreading measles, polio, and venereal disease.

By contrast, Dr. Elders, a professor of pediatrics and, for six years, the director of the Arkansas Department of Health under Governor Bill Clinton, was among a new breed of public health officials who defined their mission more broadly. She drew connections between unhealthy people and unhealthy social conditions, such as poverty and ignorance. And she advocated broad public reponsibility for changing unhealthy conditions.

In Arkansas, the focus of her attention was the disease and despair bred by rural poverty, which she knew intimately from her own childhood. Growing up in Schaal, Arkansas, in the 1930s, she was the oldest of eight children in a farm family living in a rickety three-room house without running water. She worked in the fields while tending the younger children every day of her life until she went off to Philander Smith College in Little Rock on a church scholarship—although not before the entire family scoured their meager cotton crop for days to raise $5 for her bus fare and food for the first day or two. After that, she had to find work for room and board.

Her family, strongly rooted in community and church, fared well in spite of its harsh circumstances, but she knew what poverty was and what it could do to people. Still she was shocked when she revisited these scenes on becoming public health director after years in the professional precincts of the medical school laboratory and class-room. Small farms no longer supported families even at a subsistence level, and the small-town enterprises that had supported and been supported by small farms could provide no employment either. Surveys of local conditions were dismaying. "Maybe the worst part," she said, "was the world of sexual abuse we uncovered and the widespread feeling among . . . young people that life was not worth living, which was connected directly with alcohol and drug use and early sexual activity."[4]

In this entire picture, it was the prevalence of teenage pregnancy that particularly enraged Elders. The spectacle of teenage girls unwit-tingly and unnecessarily throwing away through early childbirth their best chances at education, personal growth, rewarding work, and adult self-respect set her off on a campaign to reach these children before they fell off the social edge. She was further spurred in this effort by the conviction that reducing teen births, and thus the number of babies born into hopeless poverty, was the key to more general and positive change.

Her basic policy as state health director was to engage in vigorous public intervention on two related fronts. One was education. She wanted to combat ignorance about sex and its consequences with serious, scientific, age-appropriate sex education from kindergarten through high school. The second strategy was to open access to health care to children and teenagers by establishing public school–based health clinics. An important function of the clinics would be to rein-force classroom lessons with personal advice about sex practices, in-cluding the use of condoms—which the clinics would distribute. All of this would be subject to local approval, once it was approved by the

state legislature, and Elders assumed the task of winning those ap-
provals. She also supported the legality of abortion without undue
restriction.

By the mid-'80s, when Elders began her directorship, none of the
programs she advocated was new or remarkable as public policy, but
her approach to winning public acceptance of them was startling to
many. All such policies were ferociously opposed by religious conservatives. And sex education was particularly threatening because teachings about conception, contraception, and abortion brought the
tension between nature and choice in family matters into unresolvable
conflict. Thus at every public meeting where Elders promoted her program, fundamentalist groups rose in furious protest. But she was even
more furious. Eschewing temperate words and diplomacy, she defended her initiatives loudly, pugnaciously, relentlessly, in pithy language reflecting horror and outrage at the conditions she was trying to
mitigate.

> I tell every girl that when she goes out on a date, put a condom in her
> purse.
> We taught them what to do in the front seat of a car [driver education];
> now it is time to teach them what to do in the back seat.
> We would like for the right-to-life, anti-choice folks to really get over
> their love affair with the fetus and start supporting children.
> We have refused to make a commitment to solving the crisis of teenage
> motherhood because we view pregnancy as just punishment for the sin of
> premarital sex.
> In the seventeen years that abortion has been legal nationwide, it has
> had an important and positive effect on public health.[5]

Whether due to the messenger or the message, she made considerable headway during her six-year tenure in Arkansas, greatly expanding the number of rural clinics, many in public schools. In no small
part, she notes, this success was due to the constant backing and
legislative lobbying of Governor Clinton, who maintained his support
in spite of the considerable pressure and occasional risk to which this
subjected him.

One test of his constancy—an incident Elders describes in her auto-
biography—occurred at a press conference outlining a package of state
programs that Clinton would be highlighting at a national governors'

conference, Youth at Risk. In her account, the press was becoming bored with a long succession of reports from various agencies, so when she was called on, she stated simply that the health department was going to reduce teenage pregnancy by setting up comprehensive health education and school-based clinics. Then, asked if that meant distributing condoms in schools, she said, "Yes, it does. We aren't going to put them on their lunch trays. But yes, we intend to distribute condoms." This, she says, was the first Bill Clinton knew of the condom plan, and she, like everyone else present, turned to watch his reaction—which was to turn bright red and swallow hard, and then to answer questions with the statement that Dr. Elders had told him what she was about when he appointed her, and he supported her.

Later, when as president-elect he asked her to take the position of surgeon general, she reminded him, she says, that "if you do this, you will know exactly what you are getting. . . . You know I tend to say what I think"—to which he responded, "I know that for sure."[6]

So why did Bill Clinton bring her with him to Washington? This was a woman with a message that she was certain to deliver as loudly as she could, and it was a message bound to ignite the volatile emotions surrounding families, sex, and morality. Why risk this kind of trouble?

Perhaps he was thinking of his diversity pledge, or perhaps of the impressive example she set as someone who, through strong character and education, had overcome the triple threat of race, class, and sex to move from the direst poverty to high rank within the medical profession. He might have thought that as surgeon general, a position with no policy-making authority, she could not rock the boat too far. He was also no doubt aware of the growing respect for her in the public health community nationwide, and thought that her robust advocacy of policies reducing teen pregnancy and sexually transmitted diseases would be appealing to most people nationally, as they had been—in spite of strong opposition—in Arkansas.

But Washington was different. All of the country's contentions focused themselves there, most powerfully through organized lobbies with nationwide political and financial bases. The Christian Coalition, the strongest of the fundamentalist lobbies, flooded the Senate with angry letters as the Labor and Human Resources Committee prepared for Elders's confirmation hearings. She, however, ignoring the usual practice of nominees to speak only in platitudes or not at all in the weeks before their hearings, continued to offer trenchant commentary during this period.

For example: "If Medicaid does not pay for abortions, does not pay for family planning, but pays for prenatal care and delivery, that's saying, 'I'll pay for you to have another good healthy slave, but I won't pay for you to use your brain and make choices for yourself.' . . . If you are poor and ignorant, you are a slave." And later, "Single, unemployed with no job skills and on welfare, children who have children constitute America's newest slave class."[7] And, taunted in the conservative media as a "condom queen," she replied, "If I could get every teenager who engaged in sex to use a condom, I'd gladly wear a crown of condoms on my head."[8]

Her confirmation hearings were predictably rough, but with a Democratic Senate and Ted Kennedy shepherding her through it all, she assumed office in September 1993, and took her message national. The core remained the pressing need for sex education, K–12, and medical services located where people live or work or go to school. Added to this was advocacy of universal health care coverage as a right, and a comprehensive preventive approach to health care—which in itself would require the location of services in places, such as schools, that people could easily reach. But her primary focus remained the plight of teenagers experimenting with sex and subjecting themselves to the adult problems of pregnancy and sexually transmitted disease, including AIDS. And her outspoken advocacy of education, condom use, and abortion continued to provoke furious charges that she was encouraging immorality by teaching children about sex and providing the means of avoiding its unwanted consequences.

Elders also irritated her putative boss, Secretary of Health and Human Services Donna Shalala, by discarding approved speeches and giving her own, and by ignoring official schedule changes designed to keep her away from controversial occasions, such as gay rights meetings. In December 1993, she had caused a stir—and anger within the administration—when, in answer to a reporter's question about reducing crime by legalizing drugs, she replied that it might be worth studying the idea.

In June 1994, eighty-seven Republicans in Congress sent a letter to the president seeking Elders's resignation for advocacy of views "antithetical to the majority of citizens." The letter specified remarks about discrimination against homosexuals by the Boy and Girl Scouts, as well as her advice that girls take condoms with them on dates. In a news conference, Representative Cliff Stearns of Florida, the author of the letter, added to these charges her criticisms of the "un-Christian religious right," which, she had said, was "selling our children out in the name of religion."[9]

Then came the election of 1994 and the Republican takeover of the House and Senate in a seeming repudiation by voters of the early Clinton initiatives. The major complaints, as they appeared in the media, were big government—as represented by the Clinton health care plan—high taxes, and the president's failure to allay anxiety about insecure jobs and stagnant wage rates. But there was strong concern, too, about an erosion of moral values in the country and an identification of Democrats—or liberal Democrats—with a rejection of traditional values.

A *New York Times* story illustrated the conservative climate of 1994 with a picture from a Fourth of July parade in suburban Cobb County, Georgia. Men and women on a pro-family float were adorned with signs announcing, in huge letters, the ills of the age: DRUNKENNESS, HOMOSEXUALITY, IMMORALITY, VIOLENCE, LIBERALISM, LESBIANISM, SELF-ISHNESS, GOSSIP.[10]

Republicans had appealed to such sentiments in their Contract with America, which promised not only lower taxes and higher job growth but also a restoration of moral strength. Illegitimacy and teen pregnancy would be reduced, for example, by punishment in the form of severe cuts in welfare benefits. And the traditional family would be bolstered through various tax deductions and also by strengthening the rights of parents in their children's education.

Interviews in an Indiana congressional district where voters turned out a Democratic incumbent in favor of an ultraconservative Republican businessman suggested that a promised return to tradition had considerable appeal. People from both parties said they voted for the Republican candidate because he had strongly advocated "respect for authority, outlawing most abortions, knowing right from wrong, and having no truck with alternative lifestyles, particularly those of gays and lesbians."[11]

The Democrats, in the White House and in the Congress, were shattered. It looked as if the country had lurched sharply to the right and virtually declared war on the federal government, rejecting the very idea that its programs could be useful or beneficial to ordinary people. In this context, Joycelyn Elders's message calling for strong governmental involvement in health care was suddenly positioned on the far left, as its entire logic would shift significant influence over sexual relations and family life from private to public judgments, and from local communities to the state or even federal government. And her advocacy of sex education, contraception, and abortion clearly placed her on the wrong side of the heightened conflict between "values" and "immorality." A day of reckoning on her position was not far off.

On December 1, just a few weeks after the election, Elders spoke at the 1994 World AIDS Day conference at the United Nations and was asked by a psychiatrist about "prospects for a discussion and promotion of masturbation" as a means of avoiding harmful sexual contact. She reiterated her basic belief in the need for age-appropriate sex education generally, and then added about masturbation, "I think that is part of human sexuality, and perhaps it should be taught." The media did not immediately report the remark, but a week and a half later, with a news magazine apparently about to publish a story about it, Bill Clinton asked Elders for her resignation. As she remembers it, he called her and said, "I'm sorry this all is happening. But I hear there are all these remarks going on, and we can't have them. . . . We've just got so many things, and I'm sorry."[12]

Bill Clinton, as a secure governor, could take condoms when they were sprung on him, but in a conservative-besieged White House, masturbation was one stand too many. More to the point, Elders's opponents were many too many, and their voices were much too loud within the electorate to be ignored.

Unrecognized in this debacle is the way in which the weakness of liberals on the moral structure of families contributed to it. Elders had no firm ground to stand on when she was attacked as an enemy of moral values and family strength. She was in the position of advocating liberal policies on sexual practice for which a widely persuasive justification as a matter of social philosophy had not been worked out. That is, she was implicitly accepting the idea of a new moral order by advocating, for example, the use of condoms by teenagers, when condoms would not be necessary if kids were observing the old rule of sexual abstinence outside of marriage. Yet she could not clearly place this acceptance of change in a larger context that defined new family structures and strengths and supports. A liberal discourse on that subject was not available.

A missing family discourse also added to the weakness of the liberal position in the great losing debate over welfare in 1995 and 1996.

As we've seen, the central figure in that long battle was the unmarried mother, but not just any unmarried mother. She appeared most often in this saga as a teenager, usually black, who had engaged in irresponsible sex and had produced a baby she had no means to support. With the problem framed in this way, attacks on welfare were easy to mount. Why should Americans tax themselves to subsidize irresponsible, immoral behavior? Doesn't the availability of welfare encourage such behavior and further the country's descent into moral chaos?

In fact, as the welfare debate raged, the real picture of the welfare population was changing. While the rate of births to unmarried mothers was rising, births to teens were declining dramatically. Somewhat more than half of out-of-wedlock births were to adult women, and increasingly to white women who were poor. As I've said in discussing the welfare fight in chapter 2, the real problem was not located peculiarly in a narrow sector of the society. It was not primarily a problem of teenage moral deviance. It was a far more general problem, obviously more extreme at poverty levels, but still a problem that ran across class lines in a society without a social system that assures support for family stability and family care.

Kristin Luker, in *Dubious Conceptions: The Politics of Teenage Pregnancy*, argues that the welfare debate took the course it did precisely because the underlying problem is general and large—so large that most people don't want to look at it. Fixating on adolescent immorality made it possible, she says, not to see that the troubles of unmarried teenage parents "are the same ones that all Americans face: changes in the nature of marriage, in the relations between men and women, in the relations between parents and children," and all of this in a "bifurcating economy" placing extreme pressure on families with middle to lower incomes.[13]

In other words, it was not morality that distinguished poor teenagers and poor families generally from others. Social rules were in a state of flux for everyone as the ethic of choice contested traditional rules. New, out-of-wedlock family forms were developing at all income levels. The particular problem for the poor was that they lacked the means to support the families they were forming. But defending welfare in these terms was foreclosed, because there was no clear liberal alternative to the family rules conservatives were using as a moral yardstick. Liberals could argue only that when children were in need, the circumstances of their conception were irrelevant. Or they could and did countercharge that conservative legislators who quietly condoned high rates of adultery and divorce in their own ranks were hypocritical on issues of morality. But with no new family theory of their own, liberals appeared to be supporting not families but immorality—an impossibly weak political position.

Then there are questions about the state of sexual rules that apply once marriages are formed—specifically questions about adultery.

Certainly the wide acceptance of extramarital sex has reduced the degree of social significance Americans generally attach to adultery, but marriage as an institution still retains some defining moral power. That is, virtually no moral opprobrium now attaches to consensual sex between unmarried people, but present mores still condemn betrayal of sexual fidelity by a person who is married or in a committed domestic partnership.

But the political question is: Whose business is this? Does the impact of adultery on the stability of marriages make it a public issue? Is the public interest in the stability of families such that social and legal rules should penalize adulterers? Or is sexual behavior simply a matter for private emotional negotiation, and a decision to end a marriage simply a matter of private choice?

These questions popped dramatically into public view in the spring of 1997 when a twenty-six-year-old woman bomber pilot, First Lt. Kelly Flinn, faced an Air Force court-martial on charges of adultery and related misconduct. Flinn, an outstanding and much honored young officer, was herself unmarried but had had an affair with the civilian husband of another servicewoman. This behavior violated a military rule carrying penalties that could include a dishonorable discharge and prison. The reason for the rule was the importance of order and stability among military families. In other words, in the military, adultery was not simply a private matter. But the case produced a public outcry centered on two questions. Was adultery a serious enough offense to warrant the punishment it carried in the Air Force? And was the old double standard turning up again with Flinn, as a woman, being subjected to a different and higher standard of behavior than her male colleagues who had engaged in similar affairs?

Debate on the issues in the Congress, in the media, in the military, and elsewhere was confused. No public figure took a stand condoning adultery, but most expressed squeamishness about public punishment for it, especially on terms as harsh as those being proposed for Flinn.[14]

And the upshot was just as ambivalent. Air Force officials ducked the issue of family stability versus sexual choice by claiming the case did not center on adultery, as such, but on Flinn's lying about it to her superiors and disobeying orders not to communicate with her lover. For her part, Flinn, after weeks of fierce resistance, accepted a general discharge, which ended her military career ignominiously but removed the threat of prison.

What remained then, with the specter of harsh punishment removed, was the question of the double standard. And here the resolution was strongly reminiscent of the political responses to the Zoë Baird affair—a policy of gender neutrality, the same rules enforced with the same stringency for both sexes, followed by an easing of the awkward rules once they were applied to men.

In the immediate aftermath of the Flinn case, the armed services scrupulously subjected male candidates for top military jobs to an adultery test, as political nominees had been subjected to a nanny-tax test in 1993. In the course of one such review, Gen. Joseph W. Ralston, the choice of Defense Secretary William Cohen to be chairman of the Joint Chiefs of Staff, admitted to an adulterous affair thirteen years earlier. Secretary Cohen said it was a forgivable matter after all that time, but pressure from senators concerned about double standards forced the withdrawal of Ralston's candidacy. Then the next year, in July 1998, Cohen announced new rules comparable in effect to the 1994 congressional act limiting liability for nanny taxes: under new military rules, adultery would still be regarded as "unacceptable conduct" but it would not be punished unless it had some actual disruptive effect on a particular service.

So in the armed forces, the traditional family rules with respect to adultery gave way officially to the claims of choice. But in the meantime, a yet more explosive question of adultery arose when, in January 1998, the public learned that President Clinton was being accused of carrying on an affair in the White House with a young staff intern, Monica Lewinsky—and of lying about it under oath.

The sworn denial had occurred in a deposition taken as part of a sexual harassment suit brought against him by a former Arkansas state employee, Paula Jones. That case was ultimately dismissed for lack of merit—which I discuss more fully in chapter 8. But the president's denial was on the books. And a special prosecutor, Kenneth Starr, who for four years had been investigating charges of official wrongdoing by Bill Clinton as Arkansas governor and as president, added to his mandate the possible crimes of perjury and obstruction of justice arising out of the Jones case.

For eight months Starr brought dozens of witnesses before a grand jury compiling literal, not to say lurid, evidence of sexual encounters between Clinton and Lewinsky in pursuit of details that contradicted the president's sworn denials of sexual relations with her. The culmination of this effort was a referral to Congress of all such evidence, which Starr characterized as grounds for perjury and related crimes—and impeachment. Congress promptly released almost all of the material, including Lewinsky's graphic testimony, to the public.

The embarrassing presidential story, retailed by the media in daily salacious detail, both titillated and repulsed Americans as it ran throughout the year. But it also prompted a months-long discussion about the moral issues involved. Was it the special prosecutor's business, was it the public's business to make judgments about the president's sexual conduct? Was consensual sex—that is, personal choice in intimate relations—anybody's business beyond that of the people involved? What about adultery?

Polls consistently showed that few people thought that a sexual affair, adulterous or not, warranted serious punishment, certainly not impeachment—nor did lying about it under oath in a civil deposition, nor trying in other ways to cover it up. The exculpatory motif, in street interviews throughout the country, was respect for privacy in sexual matters. Over and over again reporters were told that the president's behavior was disgraceful, hurtful to his wife, harmful to his marriage, but finally a personal matter and a problem for the parties involved to handle, not the public. In other words, by the 1990s most Americans had come to regard marital infidelity as wrong, but not so wrong as to call for strong social enforcement of rules against it.

And this view ultimately carried the day politically. Bill Clinton, although subjected to the awful indignity of a Senate impeachment trial on charges of perjury and obstruction of justice, escaped removal from office when his Republican opponents could not muster even a simple majority, let alone the necessary two-thirds vote, to convict him. But underlying questions of sexual morality remained troubling, as was clear in the remarks of many senators who combined their votes to acquit the president of impeachment charges with strong condemnations of his personal conduct as "shameful" or "reprehensible" or "indefensible." The problem left open was to decide, as a matter of public concern, just how morally serious such conduct was.

Conservatives, standing by the old rules, could answer these questions, but liberals, with no new family theory formulated, could not. Is adultery only a private matter with every couple writing rules for themselves? Is this what the liberal affirmation of individual choice should mean? Or should we as a society take adultery seriously as wrongdoing but not as public business? If so, what is the wrong? What should liberals be concerned to protect? Through what means?

And how does an agnostic stand on adultery affect women? Does it bring the old double standard back in disguise? Does the social responsibility of women for family care put greater pressure on them than on men to protect the integrity of a marriage—to avoid adultery themselves or to accept it in a partner?

If questions about adultery require difficult thought about the value of marriage and family as social institutions and about the rules that should define and protect them, another set of questions is even harder to answer. These are issues concerning gay rights and particularly gay marriage. And here the element of choice becomes stark because nothing in tradition legitimates gay households; they are formed wholly as a matter of choice.

I don't want to be misunderstood here as saying that sexual orientation itself is a matter of choice, which many fundamentalist conservatives now claim. What I am saying is that gays living together as couples, forming domestic partnerships, are necessarily organizing these relations by their own choices because tradition doesn't define them.

Specifically, gay couples have to decide on sexual rules, on a division of family labor, on financial obligations, on how they will identify themselves and their relationship, and on who has what responsibility for the children that one or both of the partners may have. If they decide to have children as a couple through surrogacy, reproductive technology, or adoption, they must do so through a process of elaborate choice. And if the relation breaks down, they have another series of choices to make about the division of property and possibly about child support, child visitation arrangements, and other matters usually involved in traditional divorce.

For conservatives, and particularly fundamentalists, such an extremity of choice in the construction of families could not be further from what is right, further from the decrees of nature. For liberals, rejecting nature as the source of social order, the problem is to define what families should be, what role choice should play in their formation and dissolution, and what responsibility the society should assume for their sustenance.

The basic premise for any family theory is clear enough: it is the human need and desire for a close, continuing relationship that rests on commitment, that offers stability and the promise of mutually given care. Beyond that the task is to work on the design for a new family order—a design that respects both the importance of individual choice *and* the need for close family bonds, both women's equality *and* the obligations of family care, both the value of private family spaces *and* the public interest in social well-being.

WHAT FOLLOWS are sketches for that design and for family policies it might support.

CHAPTER 5

⬦⬦⬦⬦⬦

SOCIAL MORALITY
AND LIBERAL
FAMILY VALUES

THE FAMILY MUST BECOME a liberal issue. And the basis for a new liberal family politics should be outright, enthusiastic, unabashed support for families. But, of course, it cannot be unquestioning support for the family in its traditional form. The tradition is, in too many ways, incompatible with the fullest scope of responsible freedom for the individual. And for women, traditional family forms seriously compromise the opportunity to participate in the life of the society on terms of equality.

So liberals must continue, issue by issue, to question the tradition. But, most important, they need to identify clearly the reasons why strong families are necessary to the vitality of liberal values, and they need to work at designing new policies that express those values.

However, they must be prepared to do this against inevitable conservative denunciations framed, as they always are, in moral terms, with conservatives positioning themselves as the defenders of morality and picturing liberals as libertines abandoning it.

A new liberal family politics must reframe this old argument. It must refute the claim of conservatives to be the sole guardians of the country's morality. And the refutation must be solid, philosophic, not simply polemical.

First, liberals must insist with great clarity that, in a democracy, it is not nature but the people who define the nation's social code. Their values, carried across generations through continuous discussion, provide the basis for the society's laws and institutions. And succeeding generations necessarily revise past understandings about what is valuable and about the ways in which they can best realize basic values that endure. Obvious examples in American history are the abolition of slavery and the extension of voting rights to women, both of which represent new understandings of the meaning and requirements of the nation's commitment to equality.

With respect to families, the problem is to find a way of applying the society's basic values as historical circumstances change the way that families are able to operate. This is an important point for liberals to emphasize because conservatives tend to picture families as gliding through history in some static, universal form—the right form, following naturally the dictates of an unchanging morality. In fact, family forms have changed radically in different times and places, subject to the various forces that shape particular eras.

The most powerful shaping force, clearly, is a society's basic economic system. In agrarian economies, large extended families organized farmwork and family care through an intricate division of labor among themselves. As economies industrialized and people followed jobs to cities, kin networks dissolved and the nuclear family became the norm. At this point, increased wealth generated by industrial production supported a new division of labor for a broad middle class—men earning family wages in the workplace and women doing caretaking at home. Now, with wage levels depressed by labor-displacing technologies and low-wage workers abroad, women's earnings are needed for family support, and family structures are mutating again.[1]

But economic change is not the whole story. Almost as powerful is change over time in ideas, ways of understanding the world. This is where new understandings of women's nature and role come in, and new conceptions of sexuality more generally. Most women no longer accept the idea that fixed family forms should dictate and limit their place in the society. They want to be able to choose and shape their places as individuals, sharing in the promise of equality.

So the family has, indeed, been twisted out of its earlier shape over the past generation, as conservatives insist, but not because of the evil influence of liberals undermining the moral underpinnings of the society. It has happened because of the force of history, the force of economics, and the force of our own deepest ideals. But morality is not irrelevant here. We do have a large moral question before us. The question is: What do we, as a society, do about the stresses on families and family care that complicated historical forces have created?

IN ANSWERING this question, the major task for liberals is to set out clearly a moral base, a foundation of values, for liberal thinking about families. And since the American liberal tradition has never produced such a foundational philosophy—as we saw in the experience of Joycelyn Elders—the task is actually to construct one.

The deep philosophic challenge for liberals is to find a way to value families seriously while at the same time maintaining a strong, moral commitment to the freedom of individuals. In the old tradition, this was an unresolvable dilemma. Legal rules—on sexual relations, on abortion, on divorce—imposed heavy restrictions on individuals; and social rules, particularly on the division of labor, severely restricted the freedom of women. That is, the price for all the good that families did seemed to be a chronic compromise of freedom and equality for individuals. So liberals, putting individuals first, fell into their defensive silence on the nature, the value, and the importance of the family as an institution.

But at this point, the dilemma is solvable. The key is to recognize that the problem for the individual is not the family, as such, but conservative tradition, as such. If freed from conservative codes, the family holds potential—which exists nowhere else—to further liberal values by nurturing individuality, and sustaining it.

Privacy. First of all, families serve individuals by creating a veritable cocoon of privacy. They provide protected private spaces where individual values, tastes, and customs can flourish, where the pressures of the prevailing culture are relieved, and where people can feel comfortable with their singularity.

Historically, liberals have been uneasy about the claims of family privacy due to the conservative tradition that made everything that went on in families a private matter, including terrible domestic violence and abuse. But a liberal principle that recognizes the value of families as a shield for individuality clearly distinguishes between privacy that protects and privacy that endangers the individual. That is, the potential for abuse should not discourage liberals from open and enthusiastic support for families as zones of privacy that make space for the flourishing of personal identities.

So the family can protect and nurture through its provision of privacy. More than that, though, the very nature of a family's functions allows the individual to express a dimension of personality that other settings generally curb, and that is a desire for meaningful connection to others. But here is another point where liberal thinking about families gets stymied.

Intimate relation. As we've seen, the liberal stance on dealing with family issues has generally been to resist family claims that threaten individual freedom. In that context, it is difficult to add in the idea that what individuals want in family life are relations of close connectedness. A desire for connection seems to contradict a desire for freedom, and a position that supports both seems hard to imagine. Certainly, neither liberals nor conservatives have imagined it in any coherent way. Again, however, resolution is possible.

The contradiction between freedom and connection is not absolute. The desire for both and the need for both coexist in human beings. And a fully developed, fully humane politics—a new liberal politics— must encompass this complicated state of affairs. What liberals need to do is to imagine the family constructed by individuals as social beings, individuals seeking relation.

In a new liberal lexicon, the individual would appear not only as a self-defined, self-directed, self-sufficient person encased in the body armor of private rights but as a real-life woman or man who values autonomy and rights, *and also* wants and needs committed, responsible relation to others.

For the relational individual, the family provides a needed base for sociability, a place for the practice of an intimate interdependence, an exchange of caregiving and care receiving. It's a place for connecting, cooperating, reaching for understanding, expressing the need not to be alone in the universe. It is a place where constant, dependable care contributes to the strengths an individual needs for the fullest development of personality and talent and also respect and concern for others.

This is an idea that is appearing in interesting form in debates among legal scholars and political scientists discussing the fast-multiplying complications in family law. New questions about fathers' rights arise out of single motherhood; reproductive technologies are producing a myriad of issues from everyone's rights under surrogacy contracts to the ownership of donated sperm, eggs, and embryos held by fertility clinics; there are contests over gay marriage, gay adoption, even child custody by gay biological parents; and increasingly there are questions about the ease and terms of divorce.

The large question running through most of these issues is whether the law should simply validate individual freedom and accept whatever individuals choose to do on the basis on their own judgments—or whether a standard defining responsible family relationships should be weightier than individual choice. Some scholars take a strong stand on individual rights, arguing that family formation and family dissolution should be essentially a matter of private contract. Diametrically opposed are those who believe that the good of the society requires that the law should reflect traditional concepts defining families.

Then there is a third more complex, more realistic position evolving in current academic debate. As political theorist Mary Lyndon Shanley puts it, basing family law in a liberal society on a model of the strictly autonomous individual "takes too little account of the truth that human beings are constituted in part by relationships with others." A mature liberalism, she says, "must protect both individual rights as such and the associations and relationships that shape us and allow us to be who we are." It must understand and conceptualize "the individual-in-relationship that will allow us to speak more adequately than has been done so far about the simultaneity of human autonomy and interdependence, of freedom and commitment in social and politcal life."[2]

For liberals this idea means that their traditional support for individuals requires *simultaneous* support for families. And it also requires something of individuals. The individual-in-relation is not the individual that conservatives depict as engaging in virtually any kind of sexual or marital behavior without regard to its effects on others. Relation implies responsibility. In making the individual-in-relation the moral basis for family policy, liberals would be supporting a family system that requires clear obligations. It would be a system that individuals enter with the serious intent of engaging in sympathetic, understanding, supportive, caring, mutual responsibility for others over the long term. It would be a system that allows and supports the value of responsible individual relation.

Care and equality. Finally, as a base for a new liberal family politics, there are the combined moral values of care and equality. Putting them together, making them real, working out the thousands of variations in real lives that can support them require the close personal bonds of a family. Respect, obligation, love, loyalty, need, understanding—it is through these close connections over time that the social value of care is ultimately translated into actual giving and receiving. And it is through all of the intricate negotiations of closely connected lives that the giving and receiving must ultimately be balanced fairly among all family members.

I don't mean to suggest that families can easily realize these values or that all families ever will. But, as I've said in chapter 3, if care and equality *are* to be realized widely, families will necessarily play a crucial role. Therefore, if care and equality are liberal values, strong support for families must be a liberal cause.

WITH FOUNDATIONAL moral values for the family in privacy, intimate relation, and care and equality, the next question for liberals becomes: What kinds of family policies will best protect and promote these values?

Here is the general answer: Liberals must defy the prevailing concept of the family as an autonomous private entity wholly responsible for itself. They must insist on active social responsibility for the conditions necessary to support strong families. And to do this, they must reframe the current terms of political debate about families by shifting the focus of discussion from sexual morality to social morality—on a whole range of serious issues.

One issue at the center of debates about the family is the state of families headed by unmarried mothers. The numbers of such families have skyrocketed over the past thirty years. By the mid-'90s, about 30 percent of births in the United States were to unmarried women, up from about 10 percent in 1970 and less than 5 percent in 1940. And many unwed mothers are uneducated, unskilled, and unemployed, and are raising children who will have little chance of becoming well educated and well employed themselves.

These are the familiar facts that produced the great welfare battle that liberals lost with the passage of the welfare reform act of 1996. And as we've seen, that loss was partly due to the failure of liberals to move the welfare debate off conservative premises about sexual immorality as the heart of the matter.

What liberals should have done was to trace and challenge the connection between the rhetoric of conservatives about sex and their faith in the adequacy of the private market to supply all the resources needed for the well-being of American families. The connection is simple. Conservatives believe that the market is capable of supporting families through jobs with adequate wages, and therefore, if some families are not supporting themselves, it is their own fault for not earning enough money. And in the case of unwed mothers, the fault is sex without marriage. With marriage, the assumption goes, families can have the support of two-earner incomes, or even one high enough to support a breadwinner/caretaker division of labor. The conservative policy prescriptions, then, are a reinvigoration of the old sexual standards, and a cutoff of welfare to encourage marriage or at least to discourage out-of-wedlock births.

Liberals have been at a loss to defend against this position because they can hardly champion sexual practices that produce babies whose mothers cannot care for them adequately. This is the trap that Joycelyn Elders fell into. Seeking to forestall too-early pregnancies through sex education and school clinics dispensing condoms, she ran straight into the conservative attack on immorality—with no solid defense to fall back on.

What liberals need to do is to argue relentlessly that the conservative fixation on immorality as a prime cause of poverty depends on an economic premise that is profoundly and tragically false.

All the statistics in the world showing that families headed by married couples are better off than those with one parent only cannot demonstrate that the particular fathers of the children borne by many unwed mothers are capable of contributing to stable families. They, too, are most often poorly educated, unskilled, and unemployable except at low-wage, irregular, insecure jobs. Many young women and men in these circumstances do not expect that they can marry. They see no future based on certain employment. They form families with no clear plan for supporting them because they see no other choice except not to have families. And while such choices are often harmful for all concerned, they are based on a sad reality. The fact is that the present restructuring of work and wage levels is pushing incomes for unskilled workers well below what is necessary to support families.[3]

In short, the poverty of unwed mothers is not caused by a collapse of private morality. It is caused by the fact that the private market is not geared to support families. The conservative policy based on morality, marriage, and the market is not a pro-family policy.

A liberal pro-family policy would be explicitly based on grounds of social morality. It would consist of answers to questions about what kinds of social support families need to function well. What do they need to form secure private spaces for themselves, to provide good care for children and others in need, and to sustain long-term supportive relations among their members?

Part of the answer would be the Elders agenda, but it should be recast in pro-family terms as an effort to ensure the building of strong families, which teenagers are too young to accomplish. On this basis, the pregnancy-prevention agenda could be expanded to include, for example, educational and counseling programs starting in the preteen years, dependably organized after-school sports and activities, and vocational training and subsidized jobs for teenagers.

When prevention fails, another tack might be to help unwed fathers to assume responsible family roles. Massachusetts adopted such an approach in 1997, establishing a Commission on Father Absence and Family Support to explore potentially effective services—such as drug rehabilitation and job training—for young men unattached to the children they have fathered. But liberals must be careful of accepting unawares the conservative assumption that adding fathers to the family picture is all that is necessary, that with two parents able to work, or to divide paid work and at-home care, the market will take care of the rest. At low-income levels it will not.

The fundamental liberal pro-family policy must be to construct an economic base, an infrastructure of social support, firm enough to make long-term family responsibility possible, at all income levels. This would be a base including subsidies liberals have sought for years—for child care, health care, low- and moderate-income housing. But it should more ambitiously include direct income supports such as the Phelps and Schwarz proposals I discuss in chapter 3.

But issues surrounding unmarried motherhood are not confined to low-income families. Looking more broadly at this phenomenon, in an excellent and broadly researched study, the journalist Melissa Ludtke discovered substantial numbers of self-supporting women who had had one or more children outside of marriage in their twenties and thirties. And many of them, Ludtke found, had done so because they wanted families but had not found men who were willing or able to marry on acceptable terms.

Conservative condemnation of these choices surfaced dramatically during the presidential campaign of 1992 when Vice President Dan Quayle attacked the television sitcom character Murphy Brown—a beautiful, successful, divorced journalist who, in one season's story line, became pregnant by her former husband, decided to bear the child, and gave birth in a memorable episode with a band of her colleagues cheering her on. Quayle, in a speech calling for a return to "traditional family values," charged that Murphy Brown "mocks the importance of fathers by bearing a child alone and calling it just another 'lifestyle choice.'" And Quayle made clear that he was talking about a lifestyle favored by "today's intelligent, highly paid, professional woman."

The underlying conflict here between conservative sexual morality and liberal social morality is not a matter of money. It is a matter of equality.

In story after story that Ludtke collected, women who decided not to marry the fathers of their children spoke of one form or another of undependability or irresponsibility in these men, or an unwillingness on their part to commit themselves to a fully shared parental life. And the women, who had work lives of their own—although not all of them highly paid or professional—were unwilling to take on the complications of marriage to someone unwilling or unable to offer wholehearted support to a family. In other words, these women were not operating on the traditional assumption that it is the woman's role to take primary responsibility for families, and that women should expect and be willing to tolerate a certain fecklessness in men on family matters.

Rather, Ludtke says, many women today are wondering "whether, after the massive social, economic, and cultural changes that have transformed their lives, they can fit into the old bottle of marriage." And, she concludes, "If reformulations of marriage and parenthood do not take seriously women's altered expectations and the increasing importance of shared parenting responsibility for children, it is likely that more, not fewer, out-of-wedlock births will occur."[4] Or adoptions. This was Ludtke's eventual choice for herself, without marriage.

So what should liberals do here? At a minimum, they should not join the chorus of condemnation of single parenthood that lumps all varieties of the phenomenon into one deplorable category. Rather, they should challenge the conservative call for marriage as a blanket solution to the social ills of the day by opening a new dialogue about the meaning of marriage, given great changes in the family role of women.

One important point of the new dialogue would be the complication by liberals of the meanings conservatives attach to the value of responsibility. For example, we've seen that the term "personal responsibility" in the title of the 1996 welfare act implies an obligation of individual families to take care of themselves without public help. More recently, the term has become a rallying cry of the evangelical men's organization the Promise Keepers, which holds mass rallies calling men to renounce their sinful ways and assume full responsibility for their families. But religious leaders of the group seem to equate responsibility with a traditional role for men at the head of their families, resisting any concept of women's equality. That is, in conservative rhetoric, "responsibility" means tradition.

The problem for liberals is that the idea of responsibility sounds so good, it is hard to challenge. So the task is to make the distinction clear: for liberals responsibility in the context of marriage means the cooperative relation of equal individuals committed to caring for each other and the members of their family for the long term.

As for the problem of working out relations of equality within marriages, I would not suggest that liberals prescribe a particular formula for an equal distribution of family responsibilities. Variations in talents, tastes, predilections, health, schedules, and innumerable other factors are too great for that. But liberals must still insist on equality as a goal and could outline certain tests for measuring progress. For example, given the division of labor within the family, are the adult members equally able to pursue the nonfamily work of their choice? Or, in a narrower focus, when a child or other family member is sick, and one adult must stay home from work, who does so? Is it almost always the same person? If so, is the reason compatible with the goal of equality?

But the primary need is to keep a public dialogue going about the inevitability and the desirablity of change in the meaning of marriage and responsibility as we add to the social contract the goal of women's equality.

The same issues about marriage, and the same need to shift the debate over policy from sexual morality to social morality, arise in the increasingly contested question of divorce.

Fundamentalists and other religious conservatives have long been alarmed about the rising divorce rate in the United States over the past thirty years, but in the mid-'90s they were joined in this concern by a newly organized and highly vocal group with entirely different political roots—the communitarians.

Made up largely of intellectuals and academics troubled about social fragmentation, communitarians seek to reconceive public policy through a focus on the common good. They would make shared moral values, as opposed to individual interests and individual choice, the basis for the country's institutions and politics. Applying this approach to marriage and family, they seek to reinstate tradition as the basis for family policy in order to protect what they see as the family's primary moral mission, the provision of care for children.

Communitarian researchers have produced a blizzard of books showing that the children of divorce suffer debilitating emotional and behavioral problems at a much higher rate than the children of intact marriages. This, they argue, is not just a personal tragedy for many but a social burden, as the community must deal with the consequences of childhood trauma—often lifelong problems of drug and alcohol abuse, violence, and difficulty with personal relationships in school, at work, and in families. So, along with religious conservatives, communitarians oppose the ease and frequency of divorce, which they see as reflecting cultural values that elevate self-concerned individual choice above the moral responsibility for care. Their policy prescription is to tighten divorce law considerably.[5]

To date, the most dramatic development in this effort has been the adoption by Louisiana of a new marriage contract that restricts divorce to cases of long-term separation or provable wrongdoing, such as adultery, physical abuse, commission of a felony carrying a prison sentence, or abandonment of a spouse. Louisiana did not repeal its standard no-fault divorce law but gave couples the option to choose the new "covenant marriage" if they wanted to make a more binding commitment. The law was highly praised both by the fundamentalist Christian Coalition and by Amitai Etzioni, founder and director of the Communitarian Network.[6]

Liberals, however, have been rightly wary of these various family-strengthening moves. For one thing, much of the scholarship supporting the current alarm about the children of divorce is open to question. Research psychologist Arlene Skolnick points out that communitarian writers have depended largely on divorce studies that document post-divorce trauma in children without examining their predivorce conditions. If the available statistics are carefully analyzed, she says, they show that the major factors in a child's well-being are economic sufficiency, the positive involvement of parents in a child's life, and the absence of parental or other adult conflict of a serious kind—whether or not the parents are divorced. Judith Stacey also argues that the methodology of the antidivorce studies is skewed, that they obscure a wide range of variables that affect the welfare of children, and downplay irresponsibly the importance of economic security to the well-being of a child.

But a further problem with the communitarian antidivorce campaign is precisely its mono-focus on the welfare of children, as it leaves the position of women in families out of the reform picture. That is, preserving marriages to protect their caretaking function—without discussion of the assignment of caretaking labor—implies leaving the traditional division of roles and labor intact, with all of its built-in inequities.

These inequities can be particularly dire, as sociologist Demie Kurz demonstrates graphically, for women at low income levels where stress-produced drinking, fighting, and violence are the major causes of marital collapse. Kurz insists on the futility—not to mention the physical danger to women and children—of making divorce difficult for couples trapped in such circumstances. What these families need, she argues, is public support for child care and health care, not laws that keep a desperate couple legally joined on the spurious premise that their joint incomes will allay their troubles.[7]

In short, the issue that liberals should concentrate on is not divorce but—again—marriage. In testing present policy and designing new policy with respect to marriage, they should be asking: What conditions best support the possibility for couples to maintain long-term responsibility for care—for each other and for their family members? What kinds of public policy would promote those conditions? What specific policies are practical and possible?

Laws aimed at keeping couples in marriages they cannot sustain are not the answer. But neither is a hands-off policy that leaves individuals on their own in difficult family circumstances. As an antidote to irresponsible marriage or divorce, such measures as required prenuptial marriage counseling, or longer predivorce separations or waiting periods for couples with children, may be useful. But more important, as I've discussed above, are positive social supports for marriage partners as they carry out the demanding work of long-term relation and caregiving.

The strategy for liberals of shifting the political discussion about families from sexual morality to social morality also helps in thinking about what is at stake in perhaps the most difficult and politically charged family issue at present—the question of gay marriage. The key here, as with other issues, is to break out of the conservative framing of family issues as a conflict of nature, meaning morality, versus choice, meaning immorality.

The strongest basis for such a move is that conservatives undermine the authority of their own position by offering different readings of nature's principles.

Fundamentalist conservatives believe strongly that homosexuality, in itself, is unnatural and therefore unequivocally immoral, a biblical "abomination," as I've noted in the last chapter. And they oppose gay rights in any form. In 1997, for example, the Southern Baptist Convention called on the church's 16 million members to boycott the Walt Disney Corporation and all its subsidiaries, including Miramax Films and the ABC television network, because of gay-friendly employment policies and pro-gay messages in films and television shows.

But other theologians locate the law of nature differently. The American Catholic bishops, in a 1997 pastoral letter, made clear that their church draws a distinction between a homosexual orientation and homosexual acts. The orientation is natural, not immoral, they said, and they urged Catholic parents of gay children to accept, love, and support them. However, they reiterated the Catholic teaching that the only moral sexual acts are those that are naturally procreative, and therefore homosexual sex and, of course, marriage, are wrong.[8]

Of the other major Christian denominations, only the United Church of Christ has officially accepted the morality of homosexual practice, but most have engaged in serious debate on the subject, raising the question, at least, of revising their positions. Indeed, a committee of Episcopal bishops, charged with reviewing the possibility of "blessing same-sex relationships," reported to the church's 1997 convention that the sinfulness of such relationships was "an issue that at present is up in the air."[9]

Secular conservatives who oppose gay marriage do not necessarily regard homosexual relations as unnatural or objectionable, but they do assume that marriage is an institution with a natural structure that requires heterosexuality. The journalist David Frum, a thoughtful articulator of conservative ideas, argues that the natural purpose of marriage, the conception and careful upbringing of children, requires stability as the basic organizing principle of the institution. And the needed stability, he insists, depends on the permanent bond of a man and a woman—a bond that stems, in his view, from the natural differences between the sexes.

What we should be talking about, he says, is "how men need children (and must surrender their sexual liberty to get them) and how women need security (and must limit their personal independence in order to achieve it)." The necessary consequence, he concludes, is the "not . . . very feminist" institution of marriage, which "assigns different roles and responsibilities to husbands and wives, arising out of the different natures of the sexes." He sees gay marriage as an arrangement with no firm, natural base, a "flimsy" construction representing only the temporal choices of the parties involved.[10]

Nature clearly is not a constant guide to morality here. Its message changes with the interpreter, and it cannot supply the values the country needs for thinking about complicated questions of homosexuality.

The relevant standards for approaching the gay marriage issue, liberals must argue, are the same ones that apply to unmarried motherhood and divorce—the standards of social morality. And for liberals, this means asking whether gay marriage would support the liberal family values of privacy, responsible relation, and attentive care and equality—as elaborated earlier. However, asking the question is not to answer it, as divisions over every aspect of the issue are many—not least within the gay community itself.

Some gay activists vigorously oppose the campaign for legalized gay marriage on the grounds that the concept of family based on the lifelong emotional, sexual, and economic commitment of two people stifles other forms of vital sexual expression and other kinds of committed family groupings.

Many lesbians see marriage as fatally flawed by the continued influence of the tradition that historically placed women in a subservient position. They do not see the institution as flexible enough to encompass equality, and they want gays and lesbians to remain an outside political force working for institutional change. As activist Paula Ettelbrick puts it, "Marriage, as it exists today, is antithetical to my liberation as a lesbian and as a woman because it mainstreams my life and voice. I do not want to be known as 'Mrs. Attached-To-Somebody-Else.' Nor do I want to give the state the power to regulate my primary relationship. . . ." Legalizing same-sex marriage, she says, "would undermine our movement to recognize many different kinds of relationships."[11]

Similarly, writer Frank Browning, arguing that gay relationships were creating new and vital family forms that legalizing gay marriage would stunt, explains: "We gay folk tend to organize our lives more like extended families than nuclear ones. We may love our mates one at a time, but our 'primary families' are often our ex-lovers and our ex-lovers' ex-lovers." And he quotes the writer Edmund White, who called this development "the 'banyan tree' phenomenon, after the tree whose branches send off shoots that take root to form new trunks." Such groupings, Browning points out, have been critically important in providing care for the many homosexual men afflicted with AIDS.[12]

But yet other gay men and women strongly promote same-sex marriage, and in doing so, they have become some of the strongest voices in the present discussion about the meaning and value of marriage generally. Like the black slaves before emancipation who protested in anguish their inability to marry and keep their families intact, gay advocates of same-sex marriage are, no doubt, made more aware of the significance of the institution by their exclusion from it. By their own accounts, what they seek, in addition to the material benefits legal marriage confers, are the public legitimation of love, the experience of committed loyalty, and the protected space for intimacy that marriage has traditionally afforded.

This is an argument insistently advanced by the writer Andrew Sullivan, who often castigates fellow conservatives for failing to recognize that the many homosexuals who want to marry value the institution and would be upholding, not threatening, its strengths. Answering David Frum, whose remarks about the flimsiness of gay relationships I quoted above, Sullivan declared, "Most of us have no intention of transforming the existing institution into a responsibility-free zone. . . . We are seeking the responsibilities that marriage both recognizes and encourages. Many of us would gladly join you in helping to shore up the institution, if you would only let us in." All that is radical in such a departure from tradition, he argued, is "the radical ability to choose a partner with whom to live the rest of one's life."[13]

This formulation certainly satisfies one of the values that I argue liberals should require of families claiming public support—the principle of long-term responsible relation. Others have pointed out that another liberal principle, the value of equality in marriage, might actually be furthered by the model of gay couples who organize their lives together without predefined, socially enforced expectations concerning the division of paid and unpaid labor.[14] And as for the principle of providing attentive, long-term care, there is substantial evidence that many gay partners want to form caregiving families. Some are offering care to foster children in states that allow this. Others are seeking changes in family law so that they can adopt children. And many are raising the biological children of one of the partners.

Shifting the focus of discussion from sexual morality to social morality would allow liberals to raise considerations of this kind. However, social divisions over same-sex marriage are so deep that a great deal more public conversation is necessary before a broad liberal constituency could come to a firm and sustainable position on the issue as a matter of public policy.[15]

As a final prescription for a liberal family policy, I would cite the stand of sociologist and social critic Theda Skocpol, who argues that a new liberal politics should not only include pro-family policies as one of many agenda items but should be based squarely on family needs. And those needs are extensive.[16]

I have said that with the proliferation of low-wage jobs and the loss of unpaid caretaking labor, many families need substantial public support to operate well. And this is true not just for people in poverty but for workers well into middle-class ranks. But I would reiterate here the need of families at all income levels, from the lowest to the highest, for socially responsible changes in the structure of work.

Families need time. Families need protected space. The individuals who make up families, and who seek to establish and sustain the intimate relations that satisfy a need for human connection, need unpressured time to talk or simply to be together. The adults in a family need time to feed and bathe and listen to and comfort and teach their children. They need time to help their elders. And it won't do to try to return to the old system in which women's time was freed for all of these activities, because that was a time in which women couldn't do anything else.

To talk about the value of families means nothing, liberals should be insisting, if people do not have the time for all of the little and large exchanges that create the relations that are all a family is. And people cannot find this time if they are subject to overly demanding workplace requirements.

Families are the heart of a great society. And they are at the heart of a liberal society that values care, that respects and supports the desire of the individual for intimate relation, and that seeks through all of its institutions to advance the goal of equality for men and women.

PART THREE

◈◈◈

ADDING IN EQUALITY

CHAPTER 6

EQUAL AUTHORITY: THE MOTHERHOOD PROBLEM

EQUALITY IS A KEY MEASURE of justice for Americans, and equality for women is a just goal. But what does equality mean? If we added women's equality into families and into our national system of care, what exactly would we be doing? What would a new equality-based family-care system look like? More generally, what would equality look like?

Previous chapters have filled in part of the answer. We cannot continue to place the largest share of the country's caretaking costs on women through unpaid or poorly paid work. To move toward equality we need to redistribute those costs, with employers and taxpayers absorbing more of them in various ways, and women and men sharing at-home caretaking fairly.

Further, equality must mean equal authority for men and women in all of the policy-making, rule-making, and decision-making that shape the way the society works in all important matters—including caretaking. This means women and men sharing authority in all of our choice-making institutions—in legislatures, corporations, churches, universities, courts, hospitals, governmental agencies, the media, families, and elsewhere. And here the caretaking problem is central because the timeless needs of families and the presently structured demands of work often combine to deflect women from leadership roles.

But the conflict between women's engagement in care and their full involvement in the country's work and governance is not just a matter of double demands on their time. It goes deeper than that to stubbornly held cultural assumptions about the very nature of women, and particularly the nature of women as mothers.

THE PROBLEM OF MOTHERHOOD floats through women's claim to equal authority like a ghost. It appears not in one clear form but in shifting layers of images, feelings, beliefs, anxieties, desires, certitudes, religious convictions, needs, and interests that connect women with home and children. The same concepts, of course, connect men to the public arenas of the country's life.

These beliefs set up a sense of incongruence between the caretaking work of mothers and authority-holding. They convey the idea that the qualities needed for caretaking are not only different from, but antithetical to, the qualities needed for managing a corporation, or arguing a case in court, or deciding whether or not to bomb another country. And, in general, this tradition decrees that women should be mothers first, caretakers, not authority holders.

We've seen traces of these attitudes in the story of Zoë Baird and the nanny. Baird ran into trouble in the first place because she needed a nanny, had trouble finding one, and became a lawbreaker by hiring an illegal alien—a serious problem for an aspiring attorney general. Then there was the merit question. Her credentials seemed weak—her experience as a woman encountering the nation's care crisis firsthand was not credited as important. But she also ran into the invisible barrier of stereotypes. She was a woman. She was young. She was the mother of a young child. She did not fit the prevailing idea of an attorney general, an authority figure, a holder of wide power.

What is significant about Baird's case is that it was not an isolated phenomenon. In fact, it signaled the onset of similar flare-ups throughout the 1990s as women made increasingly insistent claims to authority in areas strongly identified with men—in business, in government, in the military, in the churches. And the flare-ups are significant, as they mark the spots where old ideas continue to block women's claims to equality—the precise spots where liberals need to focus a new conversation.

Front and center in this field of dissonance is, without question, Hillary Rodham Clinton. A woman the equal of her husband in education and professional, if not political, status, deeply involved with him in the world of public policy, strong-minded and articulate, she was a disturbing figure as a presidential wife. She simply did not fit the traditional supportive role of wife-mother-caretaker. She was all of those things, but she had also been a practicing lawyer, a litigator in a private firm, and an active participant as an attorney in public interest organizations. She served for years on the boards of the Legal Services Corporation and the Children's Defense Fund in Washington, and had been constantly engaged in projects promoting health care, children's services, and educational reform during her husband's tenure as governor of Arkansas.

This was the record of an activist liberal, a strong believer in the role of government as an instrument of social reform, and she arrived in Washington in 1993 determined to take an active part in shaping the Clinton administration's social policy. She refused to remain sequestered in the East Wing of the White House, where the wives of presidents had traditionally carried out social and charitable functions. Rather, she established herself from the outset in the West Wing, claiming major decision-making authority by placing herself physically in the presidential policy-making space.

The subsequent story is familiar. President Clinton appointed her and Ira Magaziner cochairs of a task force charged with devising a new national health care policy that would guarantee health insurance to all Americans. The two of them established a controversial planning process that produced a controversial plan that died in Congress in 1994 under withering attack from multiple opponents—various parts of the insurance and medical industries, small-business associations, and legions of conservatives opposed to taxing and spending generally. Then, when the Democrats lost their majorities in both houses of Congress in the 1994 elections, much of the blame fell on Hillary's far-reaching health plan and Hillary herself, and she retreated

from the front lines of policy-making to more wifely, motherly occupations. She wrote *It Takes a Village,* her book about child care, and
toured the country advocating local programs helpful to mothers and
children.

After her husband won reelection in 1996, she returned to national
policy advocacy but in a role much narrower than that of her health
care venture. On trips outside the country she gave powerful speeches
on women's rights and on the importance of women's involvement in
public life, but at home she stayed safely within the maternal bounds of
concern for child care. And she did not take charge of the issue; rather,
she stood jointly with her husband as he presented the administration's
positions and proposals for various child-care programs.

This is a story of a woman claiming authority, gaining it briefly, and
losing much of it. And an important part of the story is the powerful
public reaction—a clamorous mix of adulation, confusion, mistrust,
ridicule, and fury—that Hillary Rodham Clinton as a national public
figure produced.

Delighting young working women and liberal professionals when
she appeared on the national scene in the 1992 campaign, she was in-
stantly identified by conservatives as the very personification of what
was going wrong with American women and families. The signal point
was precisely the departure by Hillary and women like her from the
proper role of wife and mother. Recall Marilyn Quayle at the 1992 Republican national convention remarking pointedly, although without
naming Hillary, that "most women do not wish to be liberated from
their essential natures as women." And that was mild.

Daniel Wattenberg in *The American Spectator* called Hillary "the
Winnie Mandela of American politics," then compared her to Lady
Macbeth in "consuming ambition, inflexibility of purpose, domination
of a pliable husband, and an unsettling lack of tender human feeling,
along with the affluent feminist's contempt for traditional female
roles." She was, he said, one of the new "career-first moms" who don't
want "their busy days bustling from law offices to corporate board
rooms to television studios troubled by occasional pangs of conscience
for their neglected children."[1]

These sentiments were echoed in 1992 interviews with older married women who were disdainful of Hillary as "a cold, opportunistic lawyer who looks out only for herself and looks down at housewives."[2] And Geraldine Ferraro, a veteran of both vice presidential and senatorial campaigns, said that focus groups continually confirmed that attitude on the part of women who had retained the traditional role of wife and mother. Writing in support of the beleaguered Hillary Clinton in 1995, Ferraro recalled feelingly the "anger [that] bubbles up whenever the changing role of women in society is spotlighted."[3]

It was in deference to this anger and to the fear that such attitudes would hurt the Clinton presidency, as they had in the 1994 elections, that Hillary reshaped her public persona into more traditional forms. And the tactic succeeded. By 1997 she was scoring record-high approval ratings in the polls. But nothing won her greater popular support than the fierce defense she led for her husband in 1998 when he was first embroiled in the Lewinsky scandal. Later, when Congress released the full embarrassing details of the affair to the public, her affirmations of love and support, while prompting some criticism from women outraged by the president's conduct, were generally met with great sympathy and praise.

Hillary, cast in the position of the wronged wife standing by her man—as she had done in the 1992 campaign when a similar accusation arose—went zooming up in the polls. Contemplating this phenomenon, journalist Mary Leonard remarked, "It's ironic that, after a long, rough journey, her public acceptance comes not from her achievement as a lifelong politician, professional, or policy wonk. The highest marks have come through her incarnation as Good and Loyal Wife."[4]

It is ironic, but more than that, it reflects the remaining power of the idea that women are most admirable, most virtuous, most worthy of praise when they are fulfilling the supportive role of wife or mother. And the same idea defines women as least praiseworthy when they seek to enter the world of power that has always been the often unlovely province of men.

Within this circle of ideas, to be both a good wife and a serious, competitive power holder seems impossible, and that was exactly the point on which Hillary Clinton was precariously poised. To accept her as an important national authority would be—symbolically—to lose her as a wife, a supporter, a caregiver, a mother. And fear of losing the caregiving mother touched a highly sensitive nerve running through the entire society in the 1990s.

This is what is most important in the saga of Hillary Clinton: the mother question, the anxiety about motherhood, the strong feelings that push polls up and down when the identity of woman as wife and mother is in play. Those feelings are powerful and they sit right in the middle of the equality problem. For many, women's claims to fully shared authority everywhere would obliterate the meaning of motherhood. But women cannot become equal participants in all the affairs of the society if the role of mother-caregiver effectively limits their public presence.

So what are liberals to do with this problem? With what values and purposes can liberal thought work on the blockages between motherhood and equal authority? The challenge is to loosen the hold of attitudes about mothering that tend to exclude women from claiming an equal voice in the country's affairs—but without minimizing the desire of many women to be mothers, the importance of the work that they do as mothers, and the social support that they need.

The question, then, is where the overly confining attitudes lie and how they can be changed. It is always difficult to pin down the origins of a generalized cultural outlook, but the most historically influential forces behind present conceptions of motherhood are intricate combinations of economics and religion. Social critic Constance Buchanan traces the linkage of religious ideas and secular attitudes about the mother identity of women back to the sixteenth century, when modern forms of commerce, the family, and the nation-state were developing. In this era, she says, the Protestant Reformation was translating medieval Christianity into rules for the new order—"a new set of cultural beliefs about public and private that regulated and justified a new sexual division of labor familiar to our modern eye." It did this in important part, she adds, "through a set of Christian teachings about womanhood, motherhood, the proper social organization of male and female activity, and the relationship of the home to church and state."[5]

These teachings became diffused within secular cultures over time, appearing in the early years of the American republic as the idea of True Womanhood—the identification of women's true nature with domestic life, nurturance, and moral sensitivity. Women were to contribute to the society through the strength they lent to families and communities—as opposed to taking the wider public role early feminists were claiming in the nascent suffrage movement. And this conception of women's place strengthened as the industrial revolution provided an economic base for a clearly distinct division of public and private labor.[6]

In the twentieth century, and particularly with the advent of the present women's movement, the social pressures confining women to private life have, of course, fragmented. But, according to Buchanan, the conception of womanhood-motherhood still retains the moral weight of its religious heritage. Morally defined, motherhood is not just a biological or a socially useful function, it is a measure of virtue. In this realm of understanding, the good woman is the good mother. And this idea weights the kinds of choices women make about their lives or, more important, the kinds of choices many do not imagine they have.

In politics, women in all walks of life have boldly claimed the right to speak publicly—as mothers—on matters they see as affecting children. For example, the grassroots organization Women Strike for Peace, formed in 1961, had women who had never previously entered public debate demonstrating and testifying in Congress for a nuclear test ban to keep radioactive poisons out of children's milk. Women have protested wars for which their sons could be drafted and killed. They have formed mothers' groups to fight chemical contamination in neighborhood water and soil.

But, as Buchanan puts it, most women "are not seen and for the most part do not yet see themselves as full public participants." As mothers, they "are not expected, and do not yet expect, to formulate public priorities for the whole of society and assert them with authority."[7] The sense of incongruity between the two roles, the seeming conflict between them, remains strong.

The shape of the conflict is nowhere as clear as in religious institutions that continue to profess the ideal of motherhood but must now, in this age, confront the ideal of equality. Of these, the most politically significant are the fundamentalist Protestant churches and the Catholic Church.

Christian fundamentalists are emphatic in the moral duty they prescribe for mothers, explicitly renouncing equality for women as a proper goal. Beverly LaHaye, president of Concerned Women for America, a Christian women's organization with a membership of more than half a million, continually spreads the message of a rightful hierarchy: as God is the ruler of mankind, husbands are the heads of families, wives are subservient to their husbands, and children are subservient to their parents. Therefore, the good woman does not seek equality with men. Her primary nature makes her a mother. Her natural vocation is to care for others. "Unlike the worldly feminist who lives only for herself," LaHaye writes, "the Christian woman gives of herself. The two mind-sets could not be more radically opposed because the feminist wants to get all she can while giving as little as possible. . . ."[8]

The fundamentalist writer Connie Marshner warns that those who rightly choose motherhood must be on guard against pressures from equality seekers who are undermining the validity of the right social order. Our culture, she says, "is being enveloped by a miasma of anti-motherhood," which can have the pernicious effect of sowing self-doubt among at-home mothers unless they support one another in Christian communities.[9]

And the Southern Baptist Convention in June 1998 made it an explicit part of its essential beliefs that "a wife is to submit graciously to the servant leadership of her husband even as the church willingly submits to the headship of Christ." She has, according to the new declaration of faith, "the God-given responsibility to respect her husband and to serve as his 'helper' in managing their household and nurturing the next generation."[10] Similar convictions inform the messages of the secular organizations—such as the Christian Coalition, the Family Research Council, Focus on the Family, and American Renewal—that support and spread fundamentalist teaching.

In the Catholic Church, the identification of motherhood as the primary role for women has a long doctrinal history, but the opposition between motherhood and women's equality is less clearly drawn than it is on the Protestant religious right. That is, papal pronouncements in the era of the present women's movement generally affirm both the importance of equality as a moral principle *and* the rightful centrality of motherhood in women's lives—and then try to reconcile the two by defining equality narrowly or vaguely.

As early as 1971, Pope Paul VI praised the new and growing emphasis on women's equal rights but then added, "We do not have in mind that false equality which would deny the distinctions laid down by the Creator himself and which would be in contradiction with woman's proper role, which is of such capital importance, at the heart of the family. . . ." He urged legislation that would "protect [woman's] proper vocation and at the same time recognize her independence as a person, and her equal rights to participate in cultural, economic, social, and political life."[11]

His successor, John Paul II, continued this dual instruction, but with greater emphasis on the importance of motherhood, often drawing on the figure of Mary as the model for the role of women as selfless, loving keepers of the family. "In the light of Mary," he said in the encyclical *Redemptoris Mater,* the church sees in women "the self-offering totality of love; the strength that is capable of bearing the greatest sorrow; limitless fidelity and tireless devotion to work; the ability to combine penetrating intuition with words of support and encouragement." In *Mulieris Dignitatem,* a 1988 apostolic letter devoted specifically to women, his discussion of equality emphasized the complementary differences of the two sexes—the idea that men and women have different natures that require different but equally valuable and mutually supportive social roles. And this pope also strongly maintained the church's traditional opposition to contraception and abortion, thereby further identifying women with their family-based, childbearing functions.

But in spite of its centuries-old traditions and the worldwide reach of its authority, the Catholic Church could not escape the tension inevitably created, especially among Americans, by its endorsement of women's "equal rights to participate in cultural, economic, social, and political life." Doctrinal conflict erupted openly in the United States in 1975 when two thousand Catholics met in Detroit to form the Women's Ordination Conference. There women claimed the right to equal authority within the church as priests. More generally—like women in most Protestant and some Jewish communities—they were claiming equal moral authority as religious leaders, equal participation in evolving judgments about right and wrong in vastly changing times.

Two years later, in 1977, the Vatican definitively denied women's right to ordination. But in 1983, under continuing pressure to deal with issues of equality, the National Conference of Catholic Bishops in the United States authorized the preparation of a pastoral letter on women. And they organized a highly unusual process of open, grassroots consultation on women's concerns with thousands of Catholics in churches and organizations around the country. The effort ultimately failed, however, when liberal and conservative bishops could not reach agreement after working for nine years on four successive draft documents.

The first, most liberal draft, completed in 1988, had condemned sexism as a sin, called for further dialogue about contraception, urged continuing discussion about women's ordination as priests, and asked for an early decision about their ordination as deacons. By the fourth draft, in 1992, all of these positions had been dropped under conservative pressure, a long argument against women's ordination added, criticism expressed about the tendency in American individualism to deny differences between men and women, and a charge lodged against radical feminist views linking equality to sexual freedom, contraception, and abortion. But the conservative bishops, like the liberals, lacked sufficient votes within the National Conference for an endorsement of their views, and the effort ended in stalemate.

A good gauge of the significance of this failure is the success of the American bishops in addressing other divisive issues: the morality of nuclear deterrence as cold war policy; the culpability of capitalism for failures of social justice; and, as discussed earlier, the duty of Catholic parents to love and accept their homosexual children. They could reach moral consensus on these politically charged issues but could not speak with one voice on women.

The further significance of the bishops' stalemate is that it mirrors the stalemate of the society at large regarding women's claim to authority. More to the present point, the speechlessness of the bishops mirrors the difficulties that political liberals have in reaching the heart of the issue, in recognizing and taking seriously the motherhood conundrum in the center of the equality question.

What liberals *have* done is to challenge in various ways the heavy demands that overly sacralized conceptions of motherhood place on women. Activists have, of course, championed contraception and abortion as necessary to women's ability to make choices about the course of their lives. And, as discussed earlier, many liberals now seek work-family supports that would allow women with children to broaden their identities and roles beyond motherhood by working outside as well as inside the home—that is, supports generous enough to allow this as a positive choice, not just a dire necessity.

Then there are theorists who analyze and criticize the very attitudinal structures that place a mantle of exclusive virtue around motherhood in the first place. Psychologist Diane Eyer in *Motherguilt: How Our Culture Blames Mothers for What's Wrong with Society* disputes psychological theories that make the mother-child bond the determinant of all healthy—or unhealthy—development in children. She dismisses as "baby gurus" such popularizers of maternal responsibility as Penelope Leach, T. Berry Brazelton, and Benjamin Spock, who, she says, focus so heavily on the needs of children that the needs of women mothering them remain virtually invisible.[12]

The legal scholar Robin West in *Caring for Justice* makes the intriguing argument that justice in a society must include the availability to all of good care *and* that the giving of care must be organized according to principles of justice. Her concern is the obliteration of a strong sense of self in caregivers, primarily women in families, who are subjected to social requirements that they place the needs of care recipients above all else.

For caregiving to be just, she says, the caregiver must also be cared for, because unreciprocated giving creates "injured, harmed, exhausted, compromised, and self-loathing 'giving selves,'" rather than genuinely compassionate and giving individuals." That is, unstinting, unshared caregiving, which the society praises as virtuous, reflects, for West, "not a moral sensibility but a battered sense of self." It is done for approval and at the price of a woman's "own interests, ambitions, projects, and independence."

Her point is not that women should walk away from the work of caregiving but that the care system should not place undue, unjust burdens on any one group and call the assumption of that burden a moral act.[13]

Sociologist Sharon Hays also argues that an ideology of motherhood—she calls it "intensive mothering"—places excessive demands on women by making the individual mother responsible for highly attentive care attuned to every nuance of a child's development. But in *The Cultural Contradictions of Motherhood,* she adds the further complication that we now expect women to do this while also doing paid work in a marketplace organized by an ideology based on competition, efficiency, and material gain.

This is the contradiction Hays identifies. The logic of each would undermine the other, with the greater power of the market always threatening the work of the home. Yet the culture legitimates both, and, Hays finds through interviews, most women accept the demands of both. They accept the ideology of the market as properly defining what is required of them in paid work. But they continue to measure their success as mothers according to the ideology of intensive mothering, in spite of insistent market pressures on their time. Trying to satisfy both, Hays says, they constantly find themselves wanting.

Having tracked the troubling effects on mothers of the oppressive ideologies they must juggle, Hays sees no wholly satisfactory solutions. Intensive mothering demands too much of women, but its contradiction to the market is still important to the extent that it operates "to protect us all from the full impact of a dog-eat-dog world." A partial answer here, she concludes, is to make the demanding work of mothering a shared male-female obligation. But her final point is that even shared mothering would leave the contradictory ideologies in place, still unresolved—with the power balance between them still favoring the market.[14]

Where, then, do liberals go with the problem of motherhood in the middle of a new family politics based on the twin principles of care and equality? Resisting concepts that make mothers alone responsible for the healthy development of their children is a crucial first step. But a new politics must go further than that. To relax the incongruity between such concepts and women's claims to equal authority, liberals must fully grasp the reasons why intensive mothering practices remain strong—and why they should—in the face of the opposing pressures that Sharon Hays describes.

Hays raises that question herself, almost bemusedly, and the answers she gleans from interviewees come down to variations of the simple idea that children benefit from high levels of care and mothers want to provide it, as much as they can. They do not want to organize their family lives according to an ideology of efficiency. They want time and space for the unregulable workings of love, affection, and understanding.

Polls bear out this insistent belief in the value of mothering, although they also indicate the desirability to many women of nonmothering work as well. A 1997 survey by the Pew Research Center for the People and the Press reported that 41 percent of American women thought that children were best off with a mother who stayed at home. And of women who worked outside the home full-time, a majority were not sure that this was good for their children. A huge majority, 81 percent, thought mothering was harder in the late '90s than a generation ago when more mothers were at home more of the time. But nearly as many said that, given the choice, they would not opt to be completely stay-at-home mothers themselves.[15]

Here are facts that a liberal politics needs to take squarely into account: most women want children; most women have children; and most women want to take care of their children, although not necessarily all of the time, nor to the exclusion of caregiving by men.

There is a moral gravity to these facts that must become part of the liberal consciousness. Religious prescriptions may make excessive claims for the virtue of motherhood, and such claims may persuade some women to engage in a degree of caregiving that gives away the self, as Robin West puts it. But taking care of those who need it is a moral act. Mothering is a moral act. And to the extent that women have carried the mothering assignment through the centuries—however unfair its terms have been—they have acted as trustees of an ethic of care that is essential to the good society. The unethical imposition of a too-heavy burden of care on women does not diminish the ethical nature of care itself and its moral importance.

It is this ethic that liberals should embrace—an ethic of care in general but also an ethic that allows and supports a good measure of care within families, an ethic that allows room for mothering as a relation of love and personal obligation, not simply an efficient social response to need. This is what liberals should take from the tradition that associates the care of children with mothers as a moral duty. It should be an ethic of care that does not unfairly burden women, but crucially, it should be an ethic that recognizes the moral values that motherhood has represented.

Such a political stance would, without question, be difficult to assume, because the language of moral value and motherhood does not trip easily from the liberal tongue. The very word "mother" is almost embarrassing for liberals to use in any general sense. It seems to be owned by conservatives and the religious right. It conjures up images of women mopping floors and baking pies, or antiabortion protesters waving pictures of fetuses and praying outside Planned Parenthood clinics.

And the words "morality" and "values" are, if anything, even more foreign to present liberal dialogue. For one thing, religious-sounding language invites resistance from those liberals who fear any intrusion of religion into politics as a threat to individual rights. But moral references from liberals also provoke strong opposition from conservatives who deride them as exhibitions of arrogance by elites who think they know what's best for everyone. Recall that Hillary Clinton was roundly mocked—dubbed "Saint Hillary" in a *New York Times Magazine* cover story—for an early speech in which she lamented the lack of common purpose in American life and called for "a new politics of meaning." After that experience, she retreated swiftly from such themes.[16]

The deeper political significance of the language of social morality, however, is that when liberals use it, they do so to justify broad-based social programs—the New Deal, the War on Poverty, the Clintons' health care plan. And such moves call down ferocious conservative attacks on taxing, spending, and expanding big government. In times of conservative ascendancy, then, the liberal tactic has been to deny any sweeping intent to their programs, and to justify them with rational, social-scientific analysis of definable needs and practical benefits.

This choice is utterly clear in the debate over the programs for federally funded child care proposed by Bill Clinton in 1998.

As discussed earlier, the Clintons highlighted the woeful lack of good quality day care at a White House child-care conference in October 1997, and the following January the president announced a package of remedial proposals. The programs focused on various means to increase the number of day-care facilities throughout the country, increasing the training and quality of day-care workers, and helping working families with the costs of day care through the use of tax credits.

Here is the language of justification that Bill Clinton used in making the announcement: "We know that the government cannot raise or love a child, but this is not what we are supposed to do. What the government is supposed to do is help to create the conditions and give people the tools that will enable them to raise and love their children, while successfully participating in the American workplace."[17] In previous remarks on the issue, he had emphasized the importance of good child care for strong families and healthy child development but added also that "it is good for the economy and central to a productive American workforce."[18]

There are moral references here to the good of children and families, but the primary justification is a rational appeal to general social benefit in the form of a successful and productive workforce.

This may be the approach most likely to succeed in the climate of the times, but implicit in it is a serious problem for essential liberal purposes: the mix of social trouble that the child-care proposals address is far larger than the justifications offered for them. The president spoke of children, families, people, and workers, but not mothers or even women. He did not define the full dimension of the American care crisis with its pressures on women as mothers at the center of it.

Such silence about women and mothers creates a serious problem for liberals: the longer that they avoid clear talk about these large questions, the less credibility they will have as social protectors, and the less general trust in their purposes.

Conservatives quickly located this moral vacuum in the child-care debate and rushed to fill it with their own moral prescriptions. Where the president had projected tax credits for day care, Republicans proposed a credit for families that take care of their own children at home—reflecting the conviction that home care is good and, conversely, that commercial care is bad. And most also added an income cap on tax credit eligibility for child-care expenses—reflecting the conviction that government should not subsidize women leaving home for paid work if their income is not strictly necessary for family support.

Outside of Congress, conservative commentary echoed these themes. A *Wall Street Journal* editorial conjured up what "the Clintons and their allies in the multibillion-dollar child-care industry" had in mind with the day-care initiative: "great numbers of brightly lit centers where child experts stimulate infant brains by waving flash cards before their cribs." The editorial was accompanied by a long essay from a contributor who condemned the "growing practice of abandoning infants to paid strangers" given social-science confirmation "that babies raised in day-care centers and similar institutions are often emotionally maladjusted."[19]

But even the conservatives backed off from the clear moral import of their position—honoring and supporting traditional motherhood—by avoiding the language of tradition. In an apparent gesture toward women's equality—no doubt prompted by election-year nervousness about gender gaps—the Republicans, in their various proposals, did not call at-home caretakers mothers. They called them parents, as if fathers were as likely as mothers to be the at-home caregiver. For example, Idaho senator Larry Craig, chair of the Senate Republican Policy Committee, declared, "The government should not discriminate against parents who decide to stay home and take care of their kids." And, similarly, Representative Bill Archer of Texas, chair of the House Ways and Means Committee, insisted that "we must focus more on the needs of parents who raise their own children in their own homes."[20]

So, in this late-'90s round of debate, both liberals and conservatives back off an explicit political discussion about where we want to fit mothering in our national system of care. Both come up against the tension between traditional concepts of motherhood and the new claims to women's equality and cannot figure out a way to deal with it. Both employ a rhetorical gesture, the use of gender-neutral language—parents, not mothers and fathers—to convey respect for women's equality.

This is a tactic that legal scholar Martha Fineman criticizes vehemently as producing what she calls "the neutered mother." When we base law and policy on gender-neutral presumptions, she says, the real-life fact that mothers do far more child care than fathers goes unrecognized and unsupported. The result is economic inequality for women who bear the legally invisible costs of unpaid care, and often inadequate care for children if there is inadequate time and money for good care. Fineman's argument is that we need to recognize, rhetorically and legally, the *fact* of mothering and the *value* of mothering, not to confine women in that role but to assure full-fledged social support for it.[21]

Paradoxically, it is public recognition of the importance of motherhood that will be necessary to dispel the sense of incongruity between mothering and exercising worldly authority. Making what mothers do a clear contribution to the general welfare, a kind of public act, reduces the almost mystical aura that surrounds the mother as a figure out of public sight, deep in the private realm. There is great comfort in imagining her there, standing, if only symbolically, as an unstinting giver of care. This is the figure that stands in the way of widespread acceptance of women as full-fledged public actors, initiators of policy, decision makers. The fear is that without the ever-giving mother in place, we lose the assurance of love, protection, and care. Only by moving that assurance into the center of the society, as a set of public values that include support for the mothering of children, can we free women from their long entrapment as sole carriers of those values. And only when they are released from the practical and symbolic role as sole caregiver will women be free—practically and symbolically—to become equal participants in all of the country's affairs.

◈

BUT REWRITING THE MEANING of motherhood reduces only part of the cultural incongruity between motherhood and women's equal authority. There is also the related problem of inherited concepts of authority as essentially masculine—and some substantial rewriting to be done by liberals on that score.

CHAPTER 7

EQUAL AUTHORITY:
THE WARRIOR
PROBLEM

ON THE OTHER SIDE of the motherhood problem for women claimants to equal authority stands the warrior, the symbol of resolute strength, the guarantor of protection and security in a dangerous world. Long tradition, with remnants still alive in the United States at the end of the twentieth century, assigns social and political authority not to warriors as such but to the warrior virtues—toughness, courage, vigor, stamina, fortitude, solidity, singleness of purpose, decisiveness in the face of danger. Behind the tradition lies an ancient assumption that such virtues in a society's leaders are necessary to its survival, stability, and prosperity. The result has been the creation of the warrior-citizen as the legitimate holder of serious authority.

For liberals, the figure of the warrior-citizen as shaper of the social order poses a double problem. The warrior's virtues are the traits of masculinity, and as such they undercut women's claims to authority at the outset. Symbolically, the good mother cannot be the good warrior. The images do not match. And, indeed, what we see at the authoritative levels of all our major institutions, public and private, are men— and generally men who project a strongly masculine image. But entrusting authority to the warrior also undercuts the possibility of making care a central value for the society. Warriors are concerned with threats to security and order. They are protectors, not caregivers.

In other words, authority understood as primarily protective works against the social claims of both women and care.

Advancing care and equality, then, depends on changes in conceptions of motherhood *and* changes in the tradition of special trust in masculinity as the mark of social and political leadership. This, of course, is a matter of nearly indescribable difficulty. Any kind of attitudinal change entails mysterious processes, and when the attitudes in question touch the meaning of womanhood and manhood, powerful reason-refracting emotions and resistances come into play.[1] Still, in the turbulent politics of the 1990s, signs of challenge to the primacy of masculine authority are discernible.

To see the signs and significance of change, however, it is necessary to look, at least briefly, to the origins and the long persistence of the warrior-citizen tradition. In the West, it goes back to the first formation of states as governing bodies in ancient Greece, and to the place of the warrior even in the earliest conceptions of democracy. For Athens, as for Sparta and the other city-states, especially as they became prosperous enough to support armies of considerable size, the warrior was crucial to survival. Chronically subject to attack by neighbors or rivals, the stronger states used their armies to gain control over others and thus strengthen themselves against threats from competitors.

This, then, is the lesson handed down to their successors from the early republics: the good citizen first of all must *be* a warrior, ready to fight for his community, its autonomy, its freedom. Even presumably peaceful democracies, history has taught, depend on the warrior's protection.

We can hear that lesson clearly in Abraham Lincoln's commemoration of the blood-soaked ground at Gettysburg: "that from these honored dead we take increased devotion to that cause for which they here gave the last full measure of devotion; that we here highly resolve that these dead shall not have died in vain; that the nation shall, under God, have a new birth of freedom, and that government of the people, by the people, for the people, shall not perish from the earth."

And we continue to see the linkage of the warrior and the citizen straight through to recent times. After World War II, African Americans and Japanese Americans asserted claims to full rights of citizenship— voting, desegregation—based on the fact that men from these groups had gone to war and many had died for the nation. In 1971, a constitutional amendment lowered the voting age from twenty-one to eighteen, proponents of the change explicitly linking eligibility for military service and eligibility for voting. In 1980, when President Jimmy Carter created instant controversy with a proposal to register women along with men for the draft, the women's movement divided on the issue. Some opposed it as an acceptance of militarist policies, but others argued that equal liability for armed service would establish women's civic equality generally.

It is clear enough, then, that the warrior-citizen of ancient Greece lives on in modern times. But there is more to be said about his particular role in the United States because that role takes an odd jump when it leaves Europe and lands here. The founders of the new American republic, after all, rejected European models of strong commanding government. The citizens of the New World, safe from the Old, were to order their affairs instead through the cumulative wisdom of private decision-making—in the market, in the family. So why should the warrior, the very symbol of state power, appear as an iconic figure in American politics? What is he doing here? Why do we need him?

The answer, paradoxically, is that belief in the natural beneficence of private authority requires him, because it requires some explanation for the failure of private systems to prevent outbreaks of serious social trouble. And it requires a means of solving such trouble.

To backtrack, things are not supposed to go wrong when the private market and the private family operate according to their own internal imperatives: for the market, the laws of supply and demand and competition; for the family, love, loyalty, and responsibility. So the explanation for serious trouble, as I've said in earlier chapters, focuses on wrongdoing, or disruptive forces distorting the private systems. And the solution for such trouble is for government to function as a vigilant guardian always on the alert to identify, remove, or control wrongdoers and disturbances. That is, the very purpose of government in a system so reliant on private authority is to operate as a transmuted form of warrior.[2]

A leader, then, must pass the warrior test: Can he rid us of our enemies, stamp out trouble, clean out corruption and waste, lick the Depression, the Nazis, the Communists, shield us from enemy missiles, get the government off our backs, wipe out deficits, welfare, and crime?

This test became particularly important after World War II when the United States assumed worldwide responsibility for resistance to the spread of Communism—and in doing so entered a nuclear arms race with the Soviet Union. In this period, any aspirant to national leadership who lacked the warrior virtues was doomed, and leaders in office were under constant pressure to maintain postures of toughness.

Adlai Stevenson, running for president in 1952 and 1956, clearly failed the warrior test—too intellectual, too witty, too indecisive, perhaps too fat—especially contrasted with the real thing in his opponent, General Dwight Eisenhower. And liberal Democrats in general suffered from the charge of being "soft" on Communism. Defending against this charge is certainly one reason John Kennedy kept and increased an American military presence in Vietnam, and why Lyndon Johnson expanded that commitment—even as it bankrupted his ambitious social programs. "Softness" also doomed the excitable ultraliberal Hubert Humphrey to defeat by the lifelong anti-Communist Richard Nixon in 1968.

In 1972, the Democrats seemed to have found in Edmund Muskie a strong, stalwart, even Lincolnesque figure to challenge Nixon. But Muskie discredited himself in the primaries by crying in public as he defended his wife against stories suggesting impropriety on her part. That was the end of his candidacy. Warriors do not cry.

Muskie, we should remember, was the particular target of the Nixon Reelection Committee's dirty tricks campaign that included the Watergate break-in. Repugnance for this abuse of power resulted in Nixon's resignation and also lifted the nonwarrior ban long enough to allow the small, soft-spoken, technocratic Jimmy Carter to be elected president. He, however, could not survive a siege of inflation combined with his failure to rescue the American embassy staff taken hostage in 1979 by the new Muslim fundamentalist government of Iran. His ineffectuality was unforgiveable, and he lost the 1980 election to Ronald Reagan, who knew from long movie experience how to play the hero's role. He hurled epithets at the Soviet Union, wiped out a communist threat in Grenada, defied American law to fight a communist government in Nicaragua, and won reelection in 1984.

Next to Reagan's image of masculine strength, his successor, George Bush, looked pale or, as was commonly said at the time, wimpy. To reverse this dangerous perception during the 1988 presidential campaign, Bush draped himself in American flags and mounted brutal verbal attacks on his opponent, Michael Dukakis, the technocratic governor of Massachusetts—who, regarding the charges as obviously ridiculous, failed to counterattack. This nonresponse only deepened Dukakis's own nonheroic image—short, intellectual, lawyerly—which he tried to reverse, at one point, by parading in an army tank. But this stunt only pointed up his hopelessly civilian persona when an overlarge helmet kept sliding ludicrously over his face.

Then in 1992, George Bush, who had just emerged victorious over Saddam Hussein in the Gulf War, sought reelection against an opponent even more egregiously unwarrior-like than Dukakis. Not only did Bill Clinton lack any claim to wartime heroics, he had been in the Vietnam years a draft avoider and a war protester. It was a record Bush cited relentlessly, especially in the last frantic month of the campaign. Clinton was unpatriotic: he had refused to fight. Clinton was untrustworthy: he had lied about *how* he had escaped the draft. Clinton was phony: a letter from the young Clinton recorded his relief at staying out of the war but on legal terms that would not look bad and blight a future political career.

Further, the entire Clinton persona was nonheroic—not tough, resolute, crisp, and commanding but open, smiling, conflict-avoiding, compromising. He was notoriously ill disciplined, a lover of junk food, a poor athlete, a womanizer, a musician, a hugger, a man who liked to please. And he had also violated conventional masculine norms by marrying a woman who was his intellectual and professional equal, who spoke in public as knowledgeably and authoritatively as he did, and who, moreover, served as the family breadwinner while he held low-paid political positions in Arkansas.

In no way did he conform to the warrior-citizen ideal described by Berkeley professor Robin Lakeoff during the campaign as "a daddy, a king, a god, a hero," or "Achilles, a champion who will carry that lance and that sword into the field and fight for us."[3]

Bill Clinton's victory marked a sharp break in that tradition, a weakening of the hold of the warrior idea. What had happened, unnoticed, was a confluence of changes in the conditions supporting and reinforcing the warrior's place in national politics.

Most obvious was the end of the cold war with the collapse of the Soviet Union in 1991. Another was the onset of radical change in the American economy—mergers, the export of jobs, technological displacement of workers, wage stagnation—creating a sense among Americans of something deeply wrong, something not easily definable or fixable, and something that George Bush, as warrior-president, seemed not to notice. And Vietnam still played a role, as for many Americans the warrior had been discredited there, or at least opened to question. That Clinton had joined in that questioning was not, after all, the kiss of death. Further, there was the fact of the women's movement, the fact of women appearing in all kinds of commercial and public places, their literal presence putting into question the rationality and the fairness of systems that excluded them from leadership.

In the midst of these shifting perceptions of the nation's needs, the warrior test was not a disqualifier. In fact, it might seem, conversely, that it disqualified the warrior who had become impotent to deal with the kinds of questions, the wholesale changes in economic and social conditions, then facing the country. It might seem that Bill Clinton's election—and reelection in 1996 against another war hero in Bob Dole—marked the end of the warrior-citizen tradition in the United States.

If that were the case, it ought to be a matter of rejoicing for American liberals, because it would signal a crack in the belief system that casts government narrowly as a tough, enemy-focused protector and regulator. It would mean diminished reliance on masculinity as a necessary mark of leadership and widened possibilities for women holding equal authority in the country. And it would mean the opening of political space for a serious politics of care.

But while Clinton's electoral victories signaled shifts in the culture supporting masculine models of leadership, his actual experience in office revealed the resilience of that culture and its protectors—and the continued need for liberals to understand and contest it.[4]

Clinton's most direct confrontation with defenders of the warrior-citizen tradition occurred when he challenged it at its very core by insisting from the start of his presidency on the equality of women in the military. This stand struck symbolically and powerfully at the identity of the warrior as masculine, in the most traditional understanding of that term. And it set in motion intense controversy—which Bill Clinton, apparently, did not expect. As was the case with Zoë Baird and Joycelyn Elders, he was promoting a liberal cause—in this case equal opportunity for women—without recognizing the thicket of broader issues in which it was embedded.

Women's claims to equality in the military predated the Clinton administration by years, and by the early '90s had generated considerable pressure. In 1990, a woman high school student, having been denied admission to the all-male Virginia Military Institute (VMI), had filed a complaint with the U.S. attorney general, and the Bush administration had begun a suit against the state of Virginia for violation of the Fourteenth Amendment's equal protection clause. In 1991, the infamous Navy Tailhook scandal—drunken assaults on women as accepted amusement at an annual gathering of naval aviators—broke simultaneously with the Anita Hill–Clarence Thomas hearings and forced the issue of sexual harassment of servicewomen out of the military closet into full public view. And at the same time, in the fall of 1991, Representative Patricia Schroeder—from her seat on the House Armed Services Committee and with the support of committee chairman Representative Les Aspin—succeeded in gaining legislation that lifted the enforced ban on women in certain combat positions and established a commission to study military policy on the matter. Then in November 1992, the George Bush–appointed and largely conservative commission recommended opening to women positions on most warships, but not on submarines, aircraft carriers, or combat aircraft, nor in infantry or armored units. The commission issued its report on election day, 1992, the point at which the cast of characters in this ongoing drama changed drastically. Bill Clinton appointed Les Aspin, a strong political advocate of women's rights, secretary of defense. A few months later, with the VMI case working its way through the federal courts, he appointed to the Supreme Court Ruth Bader Ginsburg, who, as an activist lawyer, had been primarily responsible for extending the reach of the equal protection clause in its application to women.

Further, when Chief of Naval Operations Adm. Frank Kelso retired early in 1994, having failed to conduct an effective investigation of the Tailhook matter, Clinton appointed in his place Adm. Jeremy Boorda, a determined protector and promoter of women in his service.

The new appointments mattered. One item on the Clinton agenda for the new administration's first one hundred days was action on the issue of women in combat, and coming in under the wire on April 28, 1993, Defense Secretary Aspin ordered the services to map a thorough overhaul of their gender policies. They were to begin assigning women to combat aircraft, to draft legislation ending the ban on women on warships, and to plan for the inclusion of women in field artillery and air defense combat units. Then in January 1994, Aspin cleared the way for women in a widened range of ground combat positions by rescinding the Defense Department's standing "risk rule," which excluded women from jobs classified generally as dangerous. He substituted a narrower rule defining only certain kinds of combat arenas as closed to women.

But efforts by the heads of services to move quickly on these orders ran into considerable resistance in the officer ranks, especially as placing women into training programs necessary for specialized combat assignments meant jumping them ahead of men already in line for the same training.

Nowhere were tensions higher over pressure from the White House and the Congress to accept women as warrior-equals than in the Navy. During the first full year of the new administration, women's advocates in the House and Senate, Patricia Schroeder foremost among them, provoked great resentment by holding up promotions of hundreds of Navy officers involved in either the Tailhook bacchanalia or the subsequent investigation that virtually whitewashed the affair. But it was not simply the Tailhook incident and its handling that was fueling anger and division within the Navy. Tailhook had been emblematic of a warrior culture that gloried in an ultramasculine identity and accorded the highest prestige to those who performed the most aggressive and dangerous military tasks—namely naval aviators and submarine crews. Within this culture, women were sexual playthings, to be possessed, used, enjoyed. Definitionally, women could not be warriors. They could not be equals. This was the psychological reality that Tailhook expressed. And it was a reality with considerable force behind it that stood in complete contradiction to the equal rights position of the Clinton administration—and its appointees.

Clinton chose Adm. Jeremy Boorda to deal with this volatile situation over Adm. Charles Larson, a representative of the Navy warrior class, precisely because of Boorda's long-established political skills. He was an innovative problem solver, highly attuned to the practical needs and interests of service people at all ranks. Further, he was wholly open to the inclusion of women in combat positions and, in fact, formulated the issue as simply a matter of personnel policy. "We're a profession that needs a lot of readiness, and it doesn't make sense to exclude half the population, does it?" he remarked shortly after becoming CNO.[5] In other words, combat was just a job. Anyone who could do the job should be considered for it.

But Boorda lacked a crucial qualification for the task of dismantling the base of the warrior-hero. He was not himself a warrior. Originally a seaman, he came up through the ranks to the officer corps, bypassing the Naval Academy and performing mainly in support services—on unglamorous surface ships and in organizational work in Washington. Focused always on the welfare of all naval personnel from top to bottom, he preached a doctrine of "one-on-one leadership" by which he meant an ethic of direct responsibility of each person for others—a nonheroic ethic of cooperation and caretaking. Furthermore, his own official stock-in-trade was quick action, informality, a breezy disregard for military hierarchy, and a healthy regard for political power, which he sought to palliate through assiduous networking.

He was, therefore, in spite of proven abilities as an administrator and considerable personal charm, a figure held in certain suspicion by the warrior class. Suspicion turned to open attack when, in a succession of cases, he acceded to the nonpromotions or resignations of top officers tainted by Tailhook or by succeeding allegations of sexual harassment. The most insistent and prominent critic on this score was James Webb, a model Marine hero with long service in Vietnam and a former secretary of the Navy in the Reagan administration. Following one contested resignation, Webb published an op-ed piece in the *New York*

Times declaring that the incident raised "serious questions about Adm. Boorda's fitness to be the Chief of Naval Operations." He meant that Boorda should stand up to political pressure and refuse to sacrifice officers with long heroic records on the altar of women's demands and complaints. Months later, in April 1996, with the intensity of such criticism mounting, Webb made a fateful speech at the Naval Academy, the breeding ground of naval warriors. There he called for a revival in the Navy of leaders "who understand the seemingly arcane concepts of tradition, loyalty, discipline and moral courage" and concluded, "It is time to give the Navy back to such leaders." He did not name Boorda but was widely understood as targeting him.[6]

Meanwhile, the staff of a private military news service was investigating Admiral Boorda's entitlement to wear certain combat insignia, which, in fact, he had removed from his ribbons some time earlier, having learned that the particulars of his service in Vietnam did not warrant them. However, on the morning of May 16, 1996, he was informed that the issue was being picked up by *Newsweek,* whose reporters were scheduled to talk with him that afternoon. Under siege within the Navy as a betrayer of warrior principles, he faced being pictured nationwide as a pretender to warrior valor. Just before the appointment, he drove himself home, went into his garden, and shot himself to death.[7]

This was a tragic ending to one battle in the epic struggle over the preeminence of the warrior-hero as rightful military leader—and as the rightful model for leadership in the society. Boorda, standing within the military as a countermodel that admitted nonwarrior virtues of decentralized responsibility and cooperation, and that included women as equal authority holders, could not prevail against deeply entrenched tradition. But the struggle was not over. The political forces behind it in the country, in the Congress, and in the Clinton administration remained in place—as did the constitutional edict of equal protection that undermined the fundamental idea of male-only leadership.

The Constitution came into play definitively only a month after Admiral Boorda's death when the Supreme Court, in an opinion by Clinton appointee Justice Ruth Bader Ginsburg, decided that the state of Virginia had no grounds whatsoever for excluding women from admission to the Virginia Military Institute—a ruling that also applied, by extension, to The Citadel, a similar state military college in South Carolina.[8]

Virginia had put forward two basic claims. The first was that women could not follow the "adversative"—meaning harsh, even brutal—training that was the VMI trademark. The school insisted that the physical and psychological stresses of a methodology designed to toughen its students were simply too tough for women. Secondly, Virginia made a "separate but equal" argument. The state had established a new program, the Virginia Women's Institute for Leadership at Mary Baldwin College, which provided military training, not through the adversative method but through a curriculum emphasizing cooperation and self-esteem—an approach the school regarded as suited to the particular attributes of women. The Citadel, similarly, had set up the South Carolina Institute of Leadership for Women at Converse College, and both states claimed that the women's programs provided education and opportunity equal to that of the established schools for men.

But as a civil rights lawyer in the 1970s, Justice Ginsburg had argued a string of cases before the Supreme Court specifically and successfully attacking sex stereotypes that legitimize discrimination against women at any governmental level. This was her issue, and she disposed of Virginia's position with scathing logic.

The linchpin of the Ginsburg reasoning was a flat denial that it was possible to categorize in general terms the abilities of men or women as respective groups. Therefore, if a state discriminated in a program or benefit on the basis of such generalizations, it was treating men and women unequally without justifiable reason. And this is what Virginia was doing with its assumption that women, as women, could not survive the adversative training at VMI. Some women couldn't, Justice Ginsburg conceded, as some men couldn't, but it was impossible to assume no women could. To base state policy on such an assumption was to violate the equal protection clause of the Fourteenth Amendment. Ginsburg then dismissed Virginia's alternative women's program at Mary Baldwin College as "a 'pale shadow' of V.M.I. in terms of the range of curricular choices and faculty stature, prestige, alumni support and influence." That was it. VMI and The Citadel had to admit women.

Another question, however—one not before the court—loomed behind the conflict over women at VMI. It is a question about the value of toughness as training for leadership. The VMI statement of mission explicitly linked military and civil leadership; its goal was "to produce educated and honorable men, prepared for the varied work of civil life, imbued with love of learning, confident in the functions of attitudes of leadership, possessing a high sense of public service, advocates of the American democracy and free enterprise system, and ready as citizen-soldiers to defend their country in time of national peril." It was to train such leaders that it subjected students to the harsh mental and physical discipline that would build stamina, toughness, self-control, and the capacity to withstand intense pressure.

But why should leadership depend on training that pits a person relentlessly against adversity? What is that leadership designed to accomplish? What is it ill equipped to accomplish? What are the military, political, commercial, and social needs of the times for which leadership is needed? Do the virtues of the adversity-defeating leader fit those needs?

Some glancing attention to the intrinsic value of adversative training surfaced in oral arguments before the Court in January 1996, when Virginia's attorney asserted that the presence of women at VMI would change the nature of the school. Justice Stephen Breyer—another Clinton appointee—responded that maybe it would change some practices like hazing or the "rat line" humiliation of first-year students, but, he went on, "The answer to that is, so what? You have to show why it's important, what it is that's so important about this hard-to-grasp, adversative kind of thing that enables you to say to women who want to go there, you can't come." Told again that women's presence would change the system, Breyer answered, "I take that as a given, but so what?"[9]

Justice Ginsburg did not pursue this line of thinking in reaching her conclusion that, due to stereotypical thinking, VMI was wrongly excluding women from its training for leadership. But, at an unexpressed level, the two sets of ideas come together. The "hard-to-grasp . . . kind of thing" that Justice Breyer was trying to fathom was a belief system that equates traditionally conceived masculine qualities—toughness, steeliness, forcefulness—with leadership. It is a system in which the importance of these qualities is strongly reinforced by the conviction that they are the opposite of fundamental feminine traits—softness, passivity, niceness—and of greater value to the public life of the society. Further, those who hold this belief equate masculine qualities with men, purely and simply. Admitting women to VMI or The Citadel denies that belief. *That* was what Justice Ginsburg, in opening VMI to women, was doing. And it was the *belief,* as well as the privileges it supported, that was being defended.

But winning the right to enter a military college and, more significantly, the right to equal status with men in the nation's armed forces did not end resistance to these rights or the women who represented them. As a matter of fact, as a matter of daily experience, as a matter of advancement to positions of command, women in the military did not enjoy equal treatment.

The most obvious, not to say lurid, signal of their inequality was the chronic practice of sexual harassment—the treatment of women not as equals deserving respect but as objects of sexual prey or of outright hostility. The first women to enter The Citadel and VMI suffered severe verbal and some physical abuse before school officials gained control of the situation. And in November 1996, a new sexual harassment scandal broke in the professional military—this time in the Army.

Initial charges of rape and harassment of new recruits by their instructors at the Aberdeen Proving Ground in Maryland mushroomed quickly into thousands of complaints registered on a newly installed hot line. Further, women from all the services told investigating reporters of a high and constant incidence of harassment in spite of official policies and training programs designed to combat it. Then in September 1997, an Army panel reviewing the problem confirmed that both sexual harassment and sex discrimination were widespread throughout the service.

Here, in dramatic highlight, was what journalist Richard Rayner acutely described as "a collision of two irreconcilable ideals"—"an ancient and culturally embedded view of what it means to be a warrior" and "the irresistible force of democracy, in the sense of absolute equality."[10] The culturally embedded view of a warrior defined him as heroically, gloriously masculine, and necessarily male. But the liberal view of democratic principles requires equal opportunity for women in the military, which means that the masculine identity of the warrior is necessarily unsettled. And that disturbance provokes resistance, including harassment, which reinforces traditional sexual roles, and discrimination, which keeps women in nonauthoritative positions.

However, under strong political direction expressing the liberal value of equality, the force of change in women's status *is* irresistible. And, indeed, the same report recommended renewed commitment by Army leadership to its already established equal-opportunity program as "a doctrinal imperative."

But because the imperative in question implicates the warrior, who stands as a symbol of masculine authority generally, the idea of changing Army practices had repercussions far beyond that service. While the air was filled with the news of sex scandals, while the Pentagon conducted multiple studies, while the problem of harassment was dismissed by many as nothing more than raging hormones among young troops, while officers closed ranks to protect their positions and privileges, a political battle went on over the warrior symbol and all that it stands for.

In December 1997, a panel headed by former senator Nancy Kassebaum Baker turned in a report on sexual harassment in all the services—and set off another round of dispute by recommending greater separation of the sexes in basic training. Congressional backers of women's equality in the military rose in immediate opposition, claiming that any separation would limit future opportunities for women, as they would inevitably be regarded as less well trained than men. Retired brigadier general Evelyn Foote, predicting that separate training would also undermine the later unity of troops, remarked in exasperation, "I feel like I'm back in the early '60s. It's going backwards." But Elaine Donnelly, president of the conservative Center for Military Readiness retorted, "It *is* moving back—and why not?" She cheered the report as "a first step in reversing this failed experiment in social engineering" and hoped it would "force people to get over their fear of the feminists" and return to the male warrior tradition that guaranteed the nation's strength. To such remarks, retired Navy captain Rosemary

Mariner replied: "This overreaction is not being driven as much by concern for military readiness as by social conservatives pushing an anti-woman agenda."[11]

In June 1998, Defense Secretary William Cohen rejected the special panel's report, opting for the continuation of integrated training in the Army, Navy, and Air Force, although with more provision for privacy in barracks and latrines. But the underlying issues remained open politically. They included practical questions about women's unequal physical strength and about the sexual distraction produced by mixing the sexes in the forced intimacy of military life.[12] At a deeper level, however, was the question about women's entitlement to equal authority, not just in the military but in the society. This was the social agenda that Captain Mariner was referring to—the carryover from military to political spheres of masculine virtue as an essential element of rightful authority, of right order, of the way things are supposed to be.

The task for liberals in the midst of this quarrel is to focus clearly on the second issue—to resist the deployment of the symbolic warrior against women's claims to equal authority generally and against a serious agenda of care. This means questioning the role of the warrior in the society, defining and limiting the specific purposes for which we need warrior qualities and abilities. What are our warriors for? For what purposes do we need exceptional physical prowess and highly developed aggressive capacities?

Those questions are of immense importance simply applied to the military in the post–cold war world. Think of the confusions that arose out of the Bush administration's 1992 intervention in Somalia, where a complete breakdown of internal order had produced conditions of mass starvation. Organized as if for a standard military mission, fully armed Marines made a night landing on the beaches of Mogadishu prepared to fight their way past local militias or brigands. But there was no enemy on the shore, only TV cameras and reporters and a scattering of bewildered but welcoming Somalians. And in the subsequent weeks and months, American soldiers were engaged mainly in policing, engineering, and the logistical organization of food and medical supplies.

There *were* episodes of serious fighting with local warlords, and the worst such engagement provoked a congressional uproar that effectively ended American involvement. But overall, the military mission in Somalia was not defined by a clear-cut enemy, nor were subsequent missions to Haiti and Bosnia. And the underlying message was clear enough for those who would read it: even within the military sphere, the function of the enemy-locating, enemy-defeating warrior was changing.

The military, however, was not the only site for contestations over warrior leadership during the Clinton administration. They occurred also in political arenas and nowhere so intensely as in the White House itself, where they centered pitilessly on the president's wife. Hillary Rodham Clinton, simply in who she was, threatened the tradition of masculine leadership in the presidency in the same way that women in combat roles threatened the military hero. Claiming serious authority herself, as discussed earlier, she seemed to be an emasculating presence, and she attracted constant, vicious attack on this score. Jokes about her masculinity and her husband's femininity were legion.

In one sense, however—and not at all in the sense that the Hillary haters intended—the Clinton jokes captured an underlying reality. Bill Clinton *was* departing from the norm of dominant masculinity in leadership. His personal style alone signaled change. Eschewing the marks of dignity and aloof authority, he jogged sweatily around Washington in short shorts, appeared in public constantly, talking, chatting, explaining, dropping into colloquial Southern speech, and famously answering on MTV a teenager's question about the style of undershorts he wore.

More significant, however, was his approach to policy, the demasculinized nature of which was starkly drawn in the 1996 presidential election campaign. Bob Dole, the longtime senator and recently resigned senate majority leader, presented himself unambiguously in the mode of the warrior-citizen. He emphasized his service in World War II and the toughness of character it took to recuperate from the terrible wounds he received. He cast the troubles of the country in terms of clear-cut wrongs and wrongdoers—mainly big government and high taxes. He offered a specific prescription for removing those wrongs—a

15 percent tax cut. And he excoriated the Clinton administration as "a corps of the elite who never grew up, never did anything real, never sacrificed, never suffered, and never learned" and yet had "the power to fund with your earnings their dubious and self-serving schemes." This was a warrior's attack on the soft, spoiled, selfish usurpers of the nation's leadership.

Bill Clinton, in response, made no attempt whatsoever to outmuscle his opponent in defense of his political manhood. Very much on the contrary, he crafted the campaign discussed earlier that he and Dick Morris deliberately designed to appeal to women—the program heavily focused on families and care. And, of course, he won. With the aid of a significant gender gap he again defeated a warrior opponent. Moreover, he did so by moving away from precepts of enemy-focused control of trouble and by posing the idea—in however modest a form—of positive social responsibility for the well-being of the country's people.

Candidates for office in 1998 were quick to grasp the Clinton lesson, some adding twists of their own. Representative Jane Harman, running for governor of California, proclaimed herself a "digital" leader, which she defined as "someone who listens, interacts, improvises, and moves." This is as opposed to the old-style "analogue" leader, stuck, she said, in linear and hierarchical habits, pronouncing on policy from on high rather than building consensus for it. The code here is fairly clear. The listening, interacting, improvising leader represents a feminine departure from the old masculine model and opens the way for consensus-based activism.[13]

Novelist Fay Weldon noted a similar cultural shift in Britain. "This is the Age of the Anima," she declared. "Here in Britain, Tony Blair's New Labour Party presents itself as female, using the language of compassion, forgiveness, apology, understanding, and nurturing—qualities conventionally attributed to women." And she added, "President Clinton is, of course, no stranger to the usefulness of such associations."[14]

That usefulness was, however, disrupted by the stark facts of the Lewinsky affair, the story of old-style sexual adventuring that, for many, revealed in Bill Clinton an appalling lack of real respect for women and of commitment to real change. In this context, his use of the language of apology and forgiveness, once the affair was fully public, was cast in wholly conventional terms—the sexual transgressor seeking redemption. This was not at all an expression of a new, feminized political posture. Still, I see the disjunction between Clinton's political antimasculinism and his unreconstructed womanizing as signaling two sides of a complicated personality with both expressing something real. What the womanizing expresses *is* appalling, but it does not necessarily negate the political meaning—or significance—of his nonwarrior conduct.

Nonetheless, the new modes of feminized politics do present the danger of the wolf in sheep's clothing—men sounding like women but still themselves in charge, the rhetoric of change covering old uncaring policies. And there is danger also in assuming that an inchoate desire in the electorate for a more nurturant society is enough to displace strong resistance to such a movement.

Bill Clinton won in 1996 but not without constant criticism, by liberals among others, for feminizing and trivializing national issues. Furthermore, while he talked about care, he specified only noncontroversial issues with little on no impact on the national budget. He backed school uniforms, for example, and curbs on teenage smoking, and mechanisms allowing parents to block out TV programs featuring sex and violence. On big-budget questions—notably welfare—he gave in to conservative pressure to reduce public responsibilities.

And subsequently, with a conservative-dominated Republican Congress in place, the seemingly pro-feminine president stayed well within traditional bounds on questions of care. Even in his 1998 day-care proposal he avoided a clear call for broad social support financed by general taxation by making the program contingent on a new tobacco tax. In other words, the pressures behind the old ways—the old restrictions on the role of government, the old conceptions of the leader as a keeper of order, a protector against things going wrong, as opposed to an agent of the country's need for care—remain strong.

To move beyond rhetoric to the reality of change, liberals need to be careful of substantively empty political appeals to women, encouraging the appeals but insisting on substance. They need to be highly aware and wary of symbolic politics, particularly when the warrior comes into play—recognizing that in politics he stands for enemy-focused, not care-focused, government. Liberals need to insist, against conservative resistance, on a conception of government and of social institutions generally that actively supports humane conditions of life for the whole population, that takes care and families seriously. And, critically, they need to contest the conventional conceptions of motherhood and masculinity that continue to form attitudinal barriers against the full participation of women in the shaping of the country's affairs.

CHAPTER 8

EQUAL OPPORTUNITY: THE PROBLEM OF PRIVATE AUTHORITY

EQUAL OPPORTUNITY is the second vital key to women's equality. Combined with equal authority throughout the society, it is an essential element of women's full citizenship.

But pairing authority and opportunity runs straight into the weaknesses of the institutions that now organize our economic and social life. In order to create equal economic opportunity for women—without sacrificing good individual-sustaining, family-sustaining care—we have to create the new and complicated and expensive systems of caretaking discussed in prior chapters. We have to bring about much more widely shared responsibilities and costs of care. And there's the rub. That degree of engagement in common social projects requires a conception of public life and public authority far broader than the principles behind our present system of almost unmediated private decision-making.

Liberals, then, have not only a care problem and an equality problem but an authority problem—the problem of expanding conceptions of public authority to include forthright, deliberate responsiveness to broad public need, and specifically to the need for family care. This means broader governmental authority from local to national levels. But it also means a different conception of authority within private market institutions. The mandate of the American business world needs to be widened to include clear-cut social responsibilities, and these would necessarily include serious support for the country's care.

The present business system, as we've seen, relies on the sum total of our *private* decisions and dealings—in the market, in the family—to fulfill the American promise of freedom and equality. It limits government to the role of guarding against trouble. It denies the need for positive, policy-constructing uses of public authority, and requires policy makers to cast their purposes as the removal of a person and group, or a corruption, or a condition producing harm to our private institutions. Even Lyndon Johnson's expansive Great Society was cast as a war on poverty, in which the government would remove blockages to equal opportunity for all in the private market.

That scheme could not work to end poverty because the sum total of private market decisions cannot automatically assure equal opportunity for all, and not because abnormal blockages prevent it. The normal operation of a private market made up of players with huge disparities of power is to produce hugely disparate returns—even if everyone is playing strictly by the rules. Witness the widening gap between rich and poor in the 1990s. And, as demonstrated earlier, the normal operation of the market will not produce costly services—like good caretaking—for people who cannot pay for them.

We cannot count on the normal mechanics of the private market to produce equal opportunity for the poor. We cannot count on them to produce the care that we need. And because we cannot count on them for care, we cannot count on them to support equal opportunity for women at any income level. But belief in the efficacy of private authority limited only by protections against its clear abuse remains so strong that claiming a broader role for public authority remains stymied. And with these conceptions in place, authoritative decision makers—whether men or women—cannot create conditions of equal opportunity because the range of their authority, what they can actually decide, is too limited.

So liberals must persist in their historic role. They must throw new energies into creating wider political space for social policies. But far more consciously and deliberately than they have in the past, they need to focus on the problem of belief systems, of ideology, and this is especially true with respect to questions of care linked to women's equality. Poverty-related care issues, while unpopular with conservatives, at least make it to the table. They get discussed and to some degree acted upon in the states and in the Congress. Gender-related equality issues have a much harder time making it past ideological resistance.

On the issue of women's equal opportunity, the most insistent conservative voices are those of politically active professional women—notably members of the Washington-based Independent Women's Forum, an advocacy group founded in 1992. The ideology of the group, as social critic Wendy Kaminer points out in a discerning report on its membership and operations, is a virtually pure form of economic libertarianism.[1] In this view, the enemy of progress toward freedom and equality for all, including women, is governmental interference with the productive capacities of an unfettered market. This means that all women should need to enter the market on equal terms is a legal guarantee of equal rights—that is, legal protection against deliberate discrimination.

In a roundtable discussion conducted by *Harper's Magazine* in 1997, Anita Blair, a leading member of the IWF, provided a particularly clear reading of these ideas as she defended them against the skepticism of other participants. Challenged to justify the increasing division of workers into two tiers—the overworked and highly paid at the top; the contingent, part-time, and poorly paid (including most women) at the bottom—Blair blamed taxes and labor rules. "The reason there's this bottom tier is that government has imposed a lot of demands on business that business simply can't handle," she said. "When government says pay people X amount of money and give everybody health insurance, it severely restricts the ability of business to negotiate with workers." And it has to be able to negotiate if it is "going to exist and make money."

Blair's answer to the complaint of many women that muted hostility, if not outright discrimination, undermines their equal treatment on the job is that they should quit and find a congenial workplace "where they can feel culturally at home." The further argument is that the market will ultimately displace disrespectful treatment of women because losing good employees is inefficient and costly.

As to the undeniable fact that the percentages of women at the top ranks of the corporate world remain small nearly thirty years after women began entering the workforce in large numbers, her answer relies on individual choice. "There are women who choose not to have children and who go at it just as hard as any man. There are other women who have children and still, you know, get the nanny and do the whole full-time-worker-who's-also-a-mother thing. And there are many, many women who have a child and then say, 'I want to be with this child.' These are personal decisions."

Danielle Crittenden, another prominent figure in the IWF, goes beyond individual choice as an explanation for women leaving high-powered jobs to take care of a child, to argue that nature is likely to propel them in that direction. Women simply want to be with their children, she says, in a way that men, due to their different "genetic wiring," do not. So more women than men opt out of the fast track, and more men than women reach the top. Not only is this inevitable, she concludes, it is what a progressive society would wish: it is good for children due to "the unhealthiness of day-care-from-birth," and it does not result in inequality for women unless equality is measured only in cash.[2]

These arguments are so faulty, the conception of equality they carry so contorted, that liberal refutations are not hard to mount, and the central fallacy is the reliance on choice with respect to child care to take the equality issue off the table. That is, if women choose economic inequality, they are not unequal.

The answer, of course, is that the great majority of women have very little power in the marketplace and therefore very little real choice about whether or where they will work, or on what terms. Many must earn family income; there is no choice about it. And, as jobs are now structured, many must work such long hours that to speak of the market offering choice with respect to managing family care is ludicrous. Many who do choose to take time out for child care face retirement with reduced pensions or 401(k)s—if they have either—and reduced Social Security benefits. Under the 1996 welfare law, poor single mothers cannot choose to stay at home with their children, even if the jobs available to them pay so little and child care costs so much that they cannot sustain their families. And recall the girls whose lives Lisa Dodson describes, young girls growing up in poverty who face a virtually fixed lack of economic choice as adults due to family responsibilities that severely compromise their schoolwork, their expectations, and ultimately their marketable skills.[3] These are given, built-in, undeniable economic inequalities for women as the market now works, and liberals must keep a clear focus on them along with the larger issues of general economic inequity.

Then, of course, there are the women who work because they want to—because their work expresses a talent, or connects them to others, or provides satisfying challenges—but whose work hours and workweeks put intolerable pressure on families. The result is that many such women, who would like to be able to work, quit. To call this process of cause and effect a matter of choice is a semantic fraud. It is purely and simply a denial of equal opportunity.

But beyond specific refutations of conservative arguments about the market and its natural assurance of economic opportunity, liberals need to broaden their challenge and to question whether conservatives can claim to stand for equality at all.

Traditionally, conservatives have justified wide *in*equalities of wealth and power within the society as the natural playing out in the market of differences among people—differences in talent, education, energy, merit generally. But the reality of the market never matched the tenets of conservative theory because the more powerful have always been able to set terms for the less powerful. And now, in a globalized economy, disparities of power have become extreme. World-spanning megacorporations and financial conglomerates can override the discipline of competition not only in labor markets but also in dealings with medium- and small-scale enterprise. To assert that women, or nonunionized workers, or other economically disadvantaged groups can enter such a market as equal competitors defies reason and distorts the common meaning of words. And to claim that resulting inequalities are due to differences in merit and personal priorities is unconscionable.

To defend themselves as plausible champions of freedom *and* equality, conservatives would have to accept the necessity for extensive governmental protections. Their alternative is to stick with the free market as the necessary engine of stability and prosperity and relinquish the American promise of equality. Robert Bork in *Slouching Towards Gomorrah* argues strongly that they should do just that. He finds no reason other than envy for making any degree of economic equality a social goal, and urges conservatives to define themselves solely as champions of freedom—tempered by morality.[4]

Conservative politicans, however, shy away from accepting inequality outright. Their public debate still promotes the gospel of antigovernmentalism as the key to freedom and equality for all. And here is where liberals should pose their challenge. They should not swallow free-market rhetoric and then try to slip barely ameliorating measures through conservative defenses. They should clearly and robustly insist that claims for an unmediated free market are fraudulent and dangerous to the most basic American values. And they should insist that conservatives take a clear stand. Are they for the unfettered market or for equal opportunity? They can't have it both ways.

But refuting conservative positions is only part of the problem liberals face in challenging ideological supports for overly broad private authority. The further and more difficult task is to recognize the ways in which they themselves become trapped in the same ideological box.

Liberals, of course, do not join conservatives in their most exuberant professions of faith in the free market, but they do get tangled up in the other major component of the American belief system—the restriction of government to the policing of wrongdoing and the removal of harmful conditions. That is, in tackling the problem of equal economic opportunity for women, liberals have focused heavily on remedies for clear-cut wrongs—sex discrimination, sexual harassment, unequal pay for equal work, excessive work hours, exploitative practices generally. And they have sought various supports for women in poverty. All of these efforts are, without question, right and necessary. But it is also right and necessary to move beyond combating trouble to constructing the complex, socially supported systems for good family care that are an essential condition of women's equality. The large challenge, then, is to build a new idea base for such a system—about which, more in a minute.

First, though, the present liberal program for righting wrongs needs some attention.

The major issue for liberals seeking to establish women's equal economic opportunity has been sex discrimination in its various guises. And the major mechanisms for combating discrimination have been legislation—the most important being Title VII of the 1964 Civil Rights Act—and litigation based on federal and state constitutional provisions for equal protection of the law. But problems plague the complex and continually controversial field of antidiscrimination law. Whom should the law protect? Against what and to what extent? Can antidiscrimination laws be effectively enforced?

One issue that liberals should regard as settled, although it remains under some intraliberal discussion, is whether equality in the workplace requires literally the same treatment of both sexes—equal rights—or different treatment that takes physical differences, mainly pregnancy, into account. The liberal answer must be support for different treatment: work rules and medical insurance provisions that take account of pregnancy, childbirth, adoption, and child care, and that do not penalize women on the job for using such benefits. Otherwise women are at a systemic disadvantage that virtually precludes equality.

The objections to this position have been well aired in decades-long debate: any claim of needed difference in the treatment of women threatens to justify different treatment that harms women, that lets loose all the old stereotypes about women's weaknesses. The answer to that objection is that we have to make distinctions between good difference standards and bad difference standards. And not to do so creates really serious threats. Listen, for example, to Anita Blair discussing incidents of women losing their jobs when they became pregnant. "As a lawyer, what I find often happens is that somebody is pregnant, and she's having a terrible time of it and missing a lot of work. That person may be fired for missing work. That's not the same as getting fired for being pregnant."[5] Notice in the second sentence the pregnant woman has become a "person." Her sex has become irrelevant. Her pregnancy has become irrelevant. This allows the "sameness" standard to apply with no difficulty—except that most women do become pregnant at some point, and if our work rules do not allow for that, we are not allowing for either good care or equality as social norms. Liberals must make that allowance.

But to adopt a difference standard to combat discrimination in the workplace does not end the debate about standards. The next problem—large, difficult, ongoing—is to decide how much extra protection women need. And within that general question, the most troublesome and intensely contested issues are those concerning sexual harassment.

In an originally little noticed but now frequently cited opinion (*Meritor Savings Bank v. Vinson*), the Supreme Court in 1986 decided that the Title VII prohibition of sex discrimination in the workplace included sexual harassment. In doing so it adopted the definition of sexual harassment promulgated by the Equal Economic Opportunity Commission in 1980—sexual demands accompanied by the threat of economic retribution if refused, and unwelcome sexual behavior so serious and pervasive that it creates a hostile work environment.[6] But except for a trickle of litigation carried on by activist women's groups, this new reading of Title VII had little practical effect—until the Anita Hill–Clarence Thomas imbroglio during Thomas's Supreme Court confirmation hearings in 1991.

Hill, as a young attorney, had worked for Thomas in several federal agencies, and during this time, she told the Senate Judiciary Committee, Thomas continually subjected her to commentary on gamey sexual subjects, including vivid descriptions of pornographic movies and assertions of his own sexual prowess.

This was the first time the Senate, and the country at large, had come face-to-face with the idea of sexual harassment as a wrongful act, as something women should not have to accept and deal with as best they could individually. Although Thomas escaped sanction in the midst of what became a she said–he said dispute, attention to the problem of harassment was unquestionably enlivened. And within several years, Bob Packwood's forced resignation from the Senate for coercive harassment of women staff members and campaign workers officially stamped sexual harassment by powerful employers as an undeniable wrong.

But at a time when old sexual norms have been drastically disrupted, deciding exactly what kinds of behavior constitute harassment has been difficult—and the more so as issues of sexual equality and sexual morality are confusingly merged.

For many conservatives, harassment is not so much a misuse of power creating economic disadvantage for women as immoral behavior offending women's sensibilities. That is, they see laws against sexual harassment as a means of punishing immorality. And their ultimate interest is in reinvigorating moral conventions that, as discussed in chapters 4 and 5, would actively perpetuate women's inequality. In other words, they are not essentially interested in women's equality.

Many conservative women, however, such as members of the Independent Women's Forum, oppose harassment law for undermining equality by portraying women as too weak to defend themselves against the normal run of male behavior. All women need to do, they argue, is just say no—or yes, if they want to. This is another manifestation of equal rights as a measure of equality, another expression of the idea that women do not need special protections in the workplace. And it is another instance of equality language confounding real equality. Claiming that women can just say no turns a blind eye to the *fact* of generally unequal male and female power in the workplace, and the *fact* that many women are subjected to unwanted sexual demands or behavior that they do not have the power to control. That is, the equal rights position effectively parallels the morality-protecting conservative position by moving the harassment debate off the point of equality—in this case by implicitly denying the fact of coercion in sexual workplace encounters.

Here Bill Clinton, as president, enters the equality problem again, ignominiously this time, as the defendant in a sexual harassment lawsuit, and then, as we've seen, as the subject of a special prosecutor's investigation of his affair with a young White House intern. What appears in these episodes, shorn of the extraordinary political drama that put his presidency in jeopardy, are all the clashing confusions about wrongdoing that surround the issue of harassment.

The lawsuit (*Jones v. Clinton*) was brought by former Arkansas state employee Paula Jones, who claimed she had suffered reprisals on the job for her refusal of a one-time, noncoercive request for sex by then Arkansas governor Bill Clinton—legally although not directly her employer. The case was dismissed without trial by a federal district court judge for lack of evidence of reprisal—and also for lack of offensive conduct serious and pervasive enough to create a hostile work environment.

The legal question left hanging in this decision was whether a one-time, noncoercive sexual proposition *should* be considered sufficient grounds for charging harassment. If it isn't, serial sex seekers in the workplace presumably are free to approach a number of women at least once, a practice that could create a generally hostile workplace atmosphere. But the further question, endlessly discussed as the Jones case proceeded toward the trial that never occurred, was the president's moral culpability. Assuming Paula Jones's story was true, should Bill Clinton, like Bob Packwood, be condemned for casual extramarital sex? Should it matter morally that, unlike Packwood, he took no for an answer, using no physical force or verbal threats? And then moral questions circle back to the law: Should noncoercion matter legally? Are the moral and legal tests the same?

A similar set of issues beset the matter of the president and Monica Lewinsky, as the nature of their affair—spelled out graphically in the special prosecutor's report to Congress and Lewinsky's own grand jury testimony—raised a subtle question of harassment. As in the Jones case, there was no literal coercion on Clinton's part. Lewinsky, by her own account, delighted in the involvement and sought to prolong it after the president called it off. The question was whether her consent was meaningful given her youth and Clinton's far greater power and experience.

Here again is an entanglement of morality and harassment law. Some lawyers argue that consent or welcomeness should not be a defense to claims of harassment because it makes the youngest, least secure, least self-protective women the most vulnerable to sex-seeking superiors at work. And it is easy enough to conclude, as a moral matter, that powerful men, certainly including the president, *should* not take advantage of romantic excitement, or even sexual adventurism, in young women they employ. Still, regarding all women as too emotionally weak to give meaningful consent to sex goes too far toward invoking old stereotypes that undermine women's claims to equality.

I would argue that the defense of consent should remain in place but that the burden of demonstrating it should be heavy. By this standard there was no harassment in the Clinton-Lewinsky affair—just terrible judgment.[7]

But Bill Clinton's sexual escapades present questions that go well beyond the working out of specific legal rules to a deeper dimension of the harassment question. Clinton was a president who, far more than any other, stood for women's equal opportunity in the workplace, including the military. More than any predecessor he placed women in positions of significant public authority—a woman attorney general, a woman secretary of state, a second woman on the Supreme Court. But his apparently habitual involvement with women as sexual playmates seems a throwback to the old male-female order in which women were defined mainly by their bodies. This is behavior that seems to ratify all the old inequalities.

On one level, then, Bill Clinton seems to represent—or literally embody—the fractures in old systems that defined sex roles, the right relations of the sexes, sexual morality, marriage rules, and the rules of etiquette through which these systems worked. And recognition of this confusing state of affairs would suggest the need for highly specific harassment rules.

But on another level, the Clinton contradiction represents not temporary chaos in a changing social order but the permanent, primal fact of unruly sexual feeling, that disruptive force always at odds with the systems designed to contain it. He can—we can—honestly support an etiquette of sexual equality and yet have trouble following its rules. This means we need to recognize some degree of permanent tension in legal efforts to build equality into the workplace where sexual feelings may complicate on-the-job relationships. The best we can do with that problem is to maintain great clarity about the purpose of harassment law.

The liberal task here is obvious: to keep public debate clearly focused on the connection between harassment and equality. A strong move in that direction is the proposal by legal scholar Vicki Schultz to expand the reach of harassment law beyond literally sexual behavior to any behavior in the workplace that undermines women's equal opportunity. For Schultz this would include, for example, verbal denigration of women, physical sabotage of their work performance, refusal of adequate training or assignments, ostracism, unfair evaluation, physical threats, and false reports of mental instability or physical weakness—all common complaints creating as hostile a work environment as sexual abuse for many women, especially those in predominantly male occupations. This range of behavior, Schultz argues, has the effect of retaining a masculine identification to certain forms of work—from fire fighting to surgery—and maintaining old patterns of sex-segregated jobs confining women at the low end of the income scale. Reconceiving sexual harassment law in these terms retains literal sexual behavior as a form of harassment but as part of a broader pattern that keeps the definition of wrongdoing properly fixed on the problem of inequality.[8]

Beyond continued concern with definitions of harassment law, liberals need to keep a sharp eye on its enforcement in the workplace. And here, two Supreme Court cases decided in 1998 provide helpful guidelines, clarifying and toughening standards defining an employer's responsibility for harassment. The new standards make an employer liable for a wide range of harassing conduct on the part of employees—including patterns of offensive touching and lewd remarks, and threats of retribution for a refusal of sexual demands even if the threats were not carried out. But they also make clear that employers can avoid liability by putting in place antiharassment policies that are effectively organized and disseminated "to prevent and correct" such behavior. That the court was serious about effective enforcement of such policies was underscored by a finding of liability in one of the cases in spite of the fact that the employer had official antiharassment procedures on the books, but not in daily practice.[9]

Between the 1998 cases and a 1991 law allowing aggrieved employees both compensatory and punitive damages for harassment, the possibility of mounting legal remedies for this form of discrimination are improved and may induce greater care on the part of employers to control it. Certainly the $34 million settlement of a harassment suit by Mitsubishi Motors of America in 1998 would suggest the need for corporations to take the issue seriously.

But, as I've stated above, combating sexual harassment and other forms of sex discrimination, however effectively, can widen the scope of opportunity for women to only a limited degree. One reason is that the remedies are primarily legal and few women can marshal the resources to battle corporations in the courts. More significant, how-ever, is the fact that the major block to opportunity is not discrimina-tion. It is the care problem. This is where the American habit of targeting wrongs and wrongdoers as the key to reform trips up liberals in their quest for women's economic equality. Focused on removing discrimination from the paid workplace as it now operates, they fail to focus on the need to transform that workplace so that women's equal-ity there does not require sacrificing family care at home.

And here there are two tangled difficulties. One is to answer unwar-ranted charges by conservatives—and now communitarians—that lib-erals seeking women's equality are indifferent or even hostile to the needs of families. The other is to recognize the ways in which liberal positions on equality and family care do not fit together and are not adequate.

First, the conservative charges. Economist Sylvia Ann Hewlett and philosopher Cornel West frame them typically in a coauthored book presenting a passionate argument for policies supporting parental care. "An important strand of liberal thinking is deeply antagonistic to the parental role and function," they say. "Scratch the surface and you will find at least some folks on the left who don't particularly like marriage or children. In their view, the enormous quantity of other-directed en-ergy absorbed for families gets in the way of freedom of choice, and ultimately of self-realization. This is particularly true for women, which is why radical feminists tend to see motherhood as a plot to de-rail equal rights and lure women back to subservient, submissive roles within the family."[10] In cruder form, feminists become monstrous male-bashing, antifamily, antichild careerists, putting ego, money, and power before all else.

As the political effect of such indictments is to undermine the very concept of women's economic opportunity, liberals have to find an ef-fective way of countering them. And this proves difficult because, of course, work and family do operate at odds in the present marketplace. The point that liberals have to make is that this parlous state is not the fault of the women who are engaged in those two valuable pursuits.

But before addressing the large question of fault, I want to clear the air of static about the role of feminists in the work-family problem. Note in the Hewlett-West remarks that "liberals" in the first sentence shortly become "women" and then "radical feminists," who turn out to be the real antifamily culprits. As feminists generally figure in public discussion wildly caricatured—modern-day witches in academic lairs, full of sinister threat—this is a convenient means of linking liberals with terrible threats to the family. The necessary defense here is to set the record straight.

It is true that there was a flare-up of antifamily feminism in the early '70s when women in consciousness-raising groups first recognized the inequalities built into traditional conceptions of women's roles in the family and the workplace. Reacting to these discoveries, many women sought equality by adopting men's rules across the board, which meant putting work first and families wherever they could fit, if anywhere. But since the late '70s, when the sterility of that approach had become clear, the focus of most feminist thinking—certainly in academe—has been on conceptualizing new rules. In varying ways, and with varying approaches and conclusions, this has meant hard wrestling with what equality can mean in relation to a wide spread of complications. How should we understand the differences between the sexes? What is given by nature and what is created by changeable social norms and attitudes? How can we trace the interconnections among class, race, and sex in the perpetuation of inequalities? Why have family systems always depended on inequality, and how can we change those systems to admit new values while retaining old strengths? The point of much of this work—especially in the social sciences—has been to find ways of accommodating equality and difference, equality and care, not to conduct a war on men and families.

I can attest to this broad perspective personally, having been deeply engaged in the academic feminist community myself. I have attended countless feminist caucuses, panels, lectures, discussions, roundtables, and retreats, taught women's studies courses, served on the Status of Women Committee of the American Political Science Association, been a Fellow at the Radcliffe Public Policy Institute, written two books on women's issues and contributed to several others, and I have rarely encountered anything like the antimale, antichild, antifamily sentiments that feminists are supposed to harbor. In fact, I would challenge anyone who imagines that these attitudes dominate feminist thought in academe to try to schedule a women's studies steering committee meeting. This is what it sounds like: "I can be there for the first half hour but then I have to pick up . . . nursery school . . . Little League . . . pediatrician . . . school vacation, kids home . . . my night to cook."

Without question, most feminist thought in the last twenty-five years *has* focused on serious social change—but not change that would demonize men or obliterate families. The conservative antifamily charge against feminists has to be answered as at best misinformed and at worst malicious.

Now back to the larger question: Who or what is at fault for serious deficiencies in the care of the country's children and families generally? It is not feminism. It is not liberalism as a philosophy or a movement committed to equality. But liberals operating in the world of practical politics do bear some responsibility because they have not squarely confronted the inextricable relation between women's equality at work and family care at home. And they have not done so because they have been too deeply enmeshed in the ideology that relies primarily on private authority—that is, the market—and limits public authority to righting wrongs. To achieve equal economic opportunity for women within a system that takes care seriously and values families, we must extend the reach of public responsibility. We have to go beyond righting wrongs to the deliberate political building of a family care system that includes the value of equality.

How do we do that? The answer must come from contentious discussion among all groups touched by the problem—families at all income levels, paid and unpaid caregivers, women and men in all kinds of workplaces, employers in all kinds of workplaces, teachers, family court judges, health care providers, service workers unions. This should be a discussion in multiple venues—in businesses, unions, legislatures, professional gatherings, churches, universities, town meetings, and neighborhoods. And it should go on over time, inventing and proposing changes as needs change.

As for my own thoughts about the shape of a new American family care system, I believe it should be a public-private collaboration, but one that imposes definite responsibilities for care on the private sector. The reigning idea that the sole corporate responsibility is to create value for shareholders must be replaced by one that expands corporate obligation to include social health—and that means an obligation to support families and care.

This is a point on which Hewlett and West—utterly committed to parental care for children, if not the equality of women—are rightly vociferous. They argue that a hugely inequitable portion of the great wealth generated by American corporations is going not only to shareholders but to corporate managers—in salaries, stock options, a cornucopia of perquisites—while the share that goes to workers declines or stagnates, even in boom times. The percentage of managers in American companies, they report, is triple that in other wealthy countries, and the compensation of top-level American managers is almost twice what comparable executives receive in Germany, Japan, and Britain. As a result, they conclude, "over a twenty-year span, the wildly successful accumulation of wealth by corporate elites has combined with a wage crunch to make the United States the most unequal country in the advanced industrial world." Thus families do not have the resources to care well for their children.[11]

Various possibilities for redirecting this maldistributed income present themselves. Taxation is obviously one, to supplement low incomes (recall the Phelps plan), to subsidize more and better child care, to support early childhood education, to extend and improve home health care for elders and the chronically ill or disabled, to provide universal health insurance, to encourage extended school days and after-school programs, and to promote other humane, life-enhancing social services.

Litigation, even if too expensive as a direct means of rechanneling corporate resources, is useful as a means of dramatizing new values that challenge present practices. Recall *Upton v. JWP Businessland,* the 1997 Massachusetts case discussed earlier in which a single mother brought suit for wrongful termination of employment when she was fired for refusing to work extra hours—until 10:00 p.m. Monday through Friday and all day Saturdays for an indefinite period—because she could not adequately care for her son under those conditions. She lost the suit under state contract law, but a number of such cases could produce sufficient pressure to change such laws.

Lotte Bailyn's trial programs in major corporations provide a model for family-supportive work structures as they demonstrate that practices allowing employees more discretionary use of time bolster morale and do not decrease profits. Management professor Joyce Fletcher takes the Bailyn position a step further, arguing that extensive involvement in caretaking seems to develop relational skills that many overly bureaucratized corporations might profitably use to improve productivity. In other words, supporting time for family care could redound to the benefit of employers not just because employees would be happier but because skills learned in caretaking would enable them to organize advantageous ways of working. Perhaps, Fletcher says, "organizations intent on transformation might even include some form of family or community involvement as a necessary condition of advancement or continued employment."[12]

Still, eking out more family time from present profit patterns, while important, is not enough. The public interest in good care requires a greater commitment of corporate resources than this—perhaps for on-site day care, not to mention higher wages, adequate health insurance, and pensions.

Liberal support for the labor movement takes on new importance in this context as unions are increasingly adding provisions for family care to their contract negotiations. They are seeking, and locally gaining, for example: child-care funds for specific local needs, on-site and near-site day care, facilities for extended-hour child care, elder-care funds for services needed by the dependents of employees, long-term health care for employees and eligible dependents, paid parental and family leave, flexible work schedules, compressed workweeks, and part-time return to work after childbirth or adoption.[13]

In short, a new care system that supports women's equality will be a package, a blend of public and private, national and local, established and newly invented programs designed to fit specific needs.

What is crucial for liberals in discussions about such programs is to retain clear focus on the two words "equality" and "design."

The first key point is to insist that women's equality—in a system designed to support it—does not threaten families or children or men. Rather—in a system designed to do so—it supports relationships of intimacy, love, trust, and loyalty. As equals, men and women both could commit themselves to care for vulnerable life, whether of the newborn or the elderly. Both could deepen their capacities for empathic relationship and know the pleasure of it. Both could pay attention to their talents and not just their roles in deciding how to shape their adult lives. Sharing all of this experience could open new possibilities of friendship and intimacy between the sexes, laying the basis for lasting bonds and truly strong families.

The second key is the argument for design. We have to *create* the conditions for care combined with equality. And that deliberate design requires a new, generous conception of public authority, which in turn depends on shared concern about common values and intertwined lives. This would be, in the words of the preamble to the Constitution, a design "to promote the general Welfare."

PART FOUR

◆◆◆

OPENING NEW
POLITICAL
CHANNELS

CHAPTER 9

A BREAK IN
THE ORDER

WHAT KIND OF POLITICAL practice would we need to construct and run a society-wide system of good family care on terms of equality for women? The short answer is that it would have to be a paradoxical politics because it would have to deal simultaneously with common values—care and equality—and the deeply conflicting interests I've traced chapter by chapter. In fact, a new politics could not succeed in pursuing these values without creating conflict and then finding ways of resolving or living with it.

When I talk about conflict at this point, I mean it in several senses. One is the mix of confusion, misunderstanding, overreaching, and corruption that inevitably surrounds any complicated venture. More important, though, are conflicts arising out of honestly held interests that differ with others in ways that cannot be reconciled without loss to someone or some group. I mean more or less zero-sum conflicts, differences that cannot yield what all concerned would call a happy ending.

These are conflicts that have to be settled by negotiation—but by negotiation that, in the context of pursuing common values, recognizes moral claims. To promote good care, to promote women's equality in a particular circumstance, which interest *should* have priority? Which interest *should* give way and bear a loss to support the common goal?

The initial difficulty in conceiving of such a politics is the familiar

American practice of trying to solve problems by rooting out something going wrong that could be put right. There are in this politics many satisfactions: solving puzzles; expressing righteous anger; fixing things quickly; avoiding the pain of loss, except for those who deserve it; and perhaps most compelling, living in perpetual optimism. It is a politics that allows us to believe that there is nothing basically wrong, nothing profoundly difficult, no tragic circumstance built into our common lives. It allows us to believe that our common values will naturally prevail if we keep a close watch on the wrongdoing, confusion, incompetence, or circumstantial blockages that chronically threaten to subvert them. We've seen that it is this conception of politics, a warrior politics, that has shaped the major responses to the social troubles of the 1990s. And we've also seen that these responses have been largely ineffectual with respect to the deep dilemmas of care, of poverty and economic insecurity, and of the mutating roles of American women.

The great need is for a politics that breaks through the constraints that block generous visions of the ongoing American experiment.

As with the mixed issues of care and equality that broke through the political surface during the Clinton presidency, so did possibilities of change in the political order—although, true to Clintonesque form, their appearances were oblique, hard to decipher, or quickly muted. The first arrived in the person of law professor Lani Guinier, a black woman who, like Zoë Baird, Joycelyn Elders, and Hillary Rodham Clinton, walked onto the national stage carrying a package of complications that immediately set off intense controversy.

Bill Clinton nominated Guinier, his law school classmate and friend, to be assistant attorney general for civil rights. And he apparently did so due to her success in litigating cases under the 1965 Voting Rights Act, which mandated race-conscious districting in congressional elections to allow sizable black populations in southern states to elect black representatives. In fact, at the official nomination ceremony, he included in his praise of Guinier the fact that she had brought voting cases against him several times as governor of Arkansas.

In one sense, the Voting Rights Act itself represented a break in the old order. The point was inclusion, bringing previously unheard voices into the political process. With a seat at the legislative table, minorities who lacked the numbers to enact policy themselves could influence debate by adding to it their own views, their own experience, a direct expression of their own interests. And broadened debate, particularly when the added participants are groups that have suffered historical disadvantage, has the potential, at least, for challenging the status quo—which is, indeed, what has happened. It is the increased participation of minorities and women in national political discourse that has put proposals for widening social responsibility—for care especially—into public view.

In nominating Guinier, Bill Clinton was clearly ratifying the value of inclusion. But only several months after the Baird affair, he was almost immediately under siege by conservatives attacking Guinier for ideas that pushed the question of minority voting well beyond redistricting.

In various law review articles, she had questioned the benefits of districting alone as a means of increasing minority influence in government. In the South, she said, creating districts with black majorities resulted in more blacks elected to office, but still so few that they were routinely outvoted in legislative bodies. Her thinking, therefore, was turning toward various forms of at-large voting—such as the systems of proportional representation (PR) or cumulative voting.

In PR elections political parties win seats according to their proportion of the whole vote; cumulative systems give voters as many votes as there are seats to be filled and allow them to distribute that number in any way they choose—placing all on one candidate, or one on each, or several on several favorites.

Such systems can raise minority representation because blacks can vote strategically for blacks, women for women, and so forth, whereas in single-seat districts, majority groups are likely to win most seats and minorities, however large, disappear from sight.

Her articles also proposed legislative procedures requiring supermajority approval of bills affecting minority populations. This would mean that a minority could block legislation it didn't like. Or the majority would have to negotiate with the minority to work out a mutually agreeable solution, which, Guinier said, is the point of the process. She also said that these methods would allow any minority, not just a racial one, to gain effective representation.

None of these ideas was unheard-of. All were in practice somewhere. The mechanism of a supermajority operates, after all, in the

United States Senate, which requires a two-thirds vote to end a filibuster or override a presidential veto. And various localities use different forms of proportional representation. In my own city of Cambridge, Massachusetts, we choose the city council by a system of preferential voting—numbering votes for nine councilors in order of preference, one to nine. One side benefit of the system is that its very complexity makes it a kind of community sport—although some of the fun has gone out of it with the recent advent of computerized voting. Previously, it would take a corps of workers the better part of a week to count and distribute the votes by an intricate formula. People would drop in to watch, speculate on the winners, and gossip, and the vote counters could earn some Christmas money. Now we learn the results immediately, on the news.

The political benefits of the system, however, remain intact. In Cambridge, the competing interests are class based: powerful universities (Harvard and MIT) and a related professional cohort on the one hand, and a loose grouping of small-business people, lower- and middle-class workers, and various immmigrant and minority populations on the other—a town and gown division. The preferential system generally produces a five to four breakdown on the council. The majority shifts from time to time, but the balance is so close that the two groups are forced into perpetual—and healthy—negotiation.

But in the national arena, with race the central issue and conservatives in full alarm at the sight of liberals advancing on Washington, a calm discussion of alternative voting methods proved impossible.

The attacks on Guinier came fast and furious. The rallying cry was "quotas"—the specter of majority rule displaced by mandated numbers of minorities. The *Wall Street Journal* took the lead, headlining an enraged op-ed critique of Guinier and another nominee, "Bill Clinton's Quota Queens." Subsequent right-wing labels attached to Guinier alone included "Looney Lani," the "Czarina of Czeparatism," the "Princess of Proportionality," "Real America's Madwoman," and more generically, "a black separatist."

With such charges of radicalism filling the air, with even the *New York Times* calling Guinier's ideas "exotic legal remedies," the Senate Judiciary Committee—not yet recovered from its encounters with

Anita Hill and Zoë Baird—informed the president that his nominee could not be confirmed and that there was no point in holding hearings. Guinier pleaded for the process to go forward anyway so that she could explain to the Senate and to the country the facts of effective minority exclusion from public debate and decision-making, and the need to begin thinking about new remedies. But Clinton, telling her that he could not risk antagonizing key senators, withdrew her nomination before she had a chance to speak.[1]

Once again, Bill Clinton had touched the corner of an immensely important question—here the matter of opening public debate to constituencies, needs, and ideas of groups not often or clearly heard from—without anticipating the thick layers of trouble wrapped around it. As a southerner with long experience in state government, he had seen the problem of racial exclusions and the remedy of redistricting but apparently hadn't imagined the extension of that problem into other minority exclusions and more far-reaching responses. He certainly wasn't prepared for a debate about these matters, nor were political liberals in general.

But this is a debate that liberals need to launch because the groups and ideas now dominating public affairs are proving unresponsive to serious social troubles building in the country. And to make public responses that take the real measure of these troubles, we need to have all the groups affected by them in the debate. Liberals have to think about and propose plans for broadening the base of public discussion.

Following the trauma of harsh political attack and lack of protection from the president in 1993, Lani Guinier has turned what had been an academic project into a public crusade for widening the public conversation. "But what might such a conversation look like?" she asks. "What would a good conversation need?" Her answer is: "A collaborative environment. To have a different kind of conversation, trust and a willingness to take risks must both be possible. Most important is a different kind of public space that would create sufficient and sustained access so people could feel safe to be honest and to be able to change their minds."[2]

◈

THE GUINIER CHALLENGE to the political order flashed on the national screen for only a moment. Longer lasting, although less sharply focused, was a break in the mode of political leadership represented by Bill Clinton himself.

In the aftermath of the bitter, ugly congressional battle over the president's impeachment, it is difficult to think about Bill Clinton's leadership in any other context. Certainly many people, conservative and liberal, see Clinton as having forfeited all claim to respect as a leader by recklessly jeopardizing his political strength through sexual self-indulgence that was bound to be discovered—and then lying about it for many months. But under the clamor, the anguish, the exaggeration, hypocrisy, crude sensationalism, and occasional serious debate about the president's behavior lie important questions for the fashioning of leadership for a new politics of social responsibility.

In such a politics, leaders would be concerned with social morality. They would be concerned with the state of care in society—health care, child care, elder care, family care. They would be concerned with wage levels, with the size of the gap between rich and poor, with dignified standards of living for everyone. They would be concerned with advances toward equal opportunity and equal authority for members of historically disadvantaged groups—including, of course, women.

But new-model leaders would also recognize, as discussed above, the deeply conflicting interests in the society, conflicts that make headway toward any common goals difficult. And this means they would see as crucial the widest, most inclusive possible involvement of citizens in the design of social policy.

To make room for such a politics to operate, we have to displace notions of the leader as a civilian warrior, a keeper of order, a vigilant guardian always on the alert to identify, remove, or control wrongdoers and disturbances. As we've seen, this is a tradition that, by emphasizing masculinity, works against the goal of equal sharing in leadership by women. This is a tradition that, by focusing narrowly on limiting trouble, works against the goal of nationally valued and supported care. And because it is so heavily focused on devising problem-controlling public policies, it is a tradition of top-down leadership—the protector taking care of the people. It is a tradition that works powerfully against real participatory engagement by citizens.

And this is where Bill Clinton comes in—before the Lewinsky debacle. In his handling of the presidency, especially in the first term, he appears as a leader who departs egregiously from the warrior-hero virtues. Most obviously, he challenged the norm of masculinity represented by the military not only with his backing for women in combat but perhaps even more so with his efforts to admit gays to the armed forces. And recall that he conducted a presidential campaign focused mainly on family issues, soft issues appealing to women—and appointed large numbers of women and minorities to high offices that had previously been the domain of white men. But beyond specific policies out of keeping with warrior leadership were personal attributes and practices that indirectly defined the functions of the presidency in distinctly nonheroic ways.

One was his habit of flouting the supposed virtue of decisiveness. Bill Clinton did not, by any means, approach policy questions in the White House by setting a clear and predictably organized course. Rather he held famously long, often rambling meetings, postponing decisions, shifting positions as he heard first one side, then another, and another on a particular question. He was famous for his desire to talk with anyone, anywhere, to extend one-on-one conversations for hours, to chat, if briefly, with hundreds of visitors in the course of a day, or to call in groups of academics periodically for free-ranging policy seminars. Observing this behavior, an exasperated *Boston Globe* editorial writer declared, "In an organizational sense, President Clinton is the unmade bed of American politics."[3] It looked as if he simply didn't know what he was doing.

But in a way that was not well defined, not clearly articulated, not wholly consistent, probably not fully deliberate, the Clinton approach to policy decisions held within it a serious purpose. It was opening up room for more voices than usual to enter the conversation, even at the risk of confusion along the way.

Clinton's secretary of education and longtime friend Richard Riley expressed something like this view in a thoughtful remark to journalist Michael Kelly. "The President has a style of decision-making that is thorough and searching and multidimensional," Riley said, "and he doesn't make John Wayne kinds of decisions but instead thinks things out in a very serious way and hears all the options, and for that reason it is kind of difficult for the public to perceive the direction he is moving."[4]

In a more unexpected quarter, an architecture review, Herbert Muschamp caught the ambiguity of the Clinton style as he discussed a French architect's startling new buildings in Paris. "There is something oddly Clintonesque about the hybrid, often unresolved quality of the work," Muschamp wrote. "[Christian de Portzamparc's] buildings seem to embody a time frozen by the conflicting desires for change and a pluralistic inclusiveness that prevents change from unfolding in a clear direction."[5]

Ronald Heifetz, director of Harvard's Leadership Education Project, although not referring to Clinton specifically, argues that indecision on the part of leaders dealing with many-sided conflict is often a highly valuable strategy. In such cases, he says, holding decisions open and allowing messy arguments to go on can produce for leaders multiple stores of information that "lie scattered in the hands of stakeholders across divisions, interest groups, organizations, and communities." Further, bringing such groups into the conversation may gain their acceptance of whatever policy emerges, whereas "exclusion can . . . cause people to sabotage the process and attack authority."

In general, Heifetz proposes a theory that defines good leadership as helping a community to do its own "adaptive work." By this he means setting up processes that allow people dealing with common problems—locally or nationally or even in nonpolitical situations—to confront serious conflicts, to clarify values and priorities, and to make decisions recognizing the costs to different groups of various choices. In other words Heifetz's good leader does not resolutely impose policy from the top down but elicits its outlines from the people involved through the messy means of guiding open conversation.[6]

I would not argue that Bill Clinton's White House policy meetings amount to a full-fledged democratic model of citizen conversation. What I do argue is that Clinton's reluctance to close off policy discussion represents an awareness of complication, a respect for varied and vital interests at play in any serious matter of policy, and a need to hear from a wide range of sources. This is nondecisiveness as a participatory virtue.

Another Clinton contribution to a new mode of leadership lies in his much noted great talent for listening—real listening.

I can testify to the authenticity of this gift as I saw it myself, in some amazement, at the 1986 Martha's Vineyard meeting that I mentioned earlier. As a state governor, he was probably the most important personage at the gathering, and as someone eyeing the presidency ahead, he was no doubt there to network with theorists and activists, and also to prepare the way for future fund-raising. But in spite of his position and whatever wheeling and dealing he was there to do, he engaged himself intently in the nitty-gritty details of meetings.

I ended up in the same small break-out group as Clinton, and it was there that I witnessed what, by now, countless people who have talked with him invariably describe as his enthusiastic absorption in the moment. Throughout the weekend, he entered the discussions fully and thoughtfully, listened carefully to what others were saying, responded with ideas that took account of prior comments, not faking, really building a larger construct as we all were. He appointed himself secretary and took notes on the large easel-backed pad supplied to each group.

In short, he worked, and seemed to enjoy it, and I was surprised because I would have expected a governor to regard himself as above this sort of thing, perhaps to make an appearance, bestow a few generalities, then involve himself with others of comparable rank or importance.

But mostly I was surprised at the listening. Important people often have stopped listening and taken to pronouncing. Or perhaps they have never done much listening. It takes time, and the sorting out of disparate messages can be confusing. Also I suspect that the ego boundaries of people who become important are often not porous enough to let in much of the thoughts and concerns of others.

And here is a problem for the making of a politics of real inclusion. A capacity for listening is crucial to any practice of broadly participatory decision-making. But if listening is to be a general attribute of future leaders, their education will have to be far different from what it is now. Law schools and business schools, traditionally the training grounds for the country's leadership ranks, are currently geared to produce not listeners but adroit competitors, skillful warriors. The prized skills in these arenas are aggression, control, winning the argument, and beating all others for whatever is at stake.[7]

Clinton himself addressed the problem of this warrior mode of politics in a talk to students at Georgetown University, remarking that ". . . as we communicate more and more with people in extreme rhetoric through mass mailings . . . or thirty-second ads designed far more to inflame than to inform, as we see politicians actually getting language lessons on how to turn their adversaries into aliens, it is difficult to draw the conclusion that our political system is producing the sort of discussion that will give us the kind of results we need."[8]

Of course, Bill Clinton had strong enough warrior attributes of his own to win the presidency twice in the shark-filled waters of the present system. But to develop a politics that can respond creatively to the needs of a complicated and conflicted society, we need to look to Clinton the listener rather than the combatant as a needed model of leadership.

A further element of nontraditional leadership that Clinton exemplifies—and for which he is often mocked—is a capacity for empathy. He has always seemed to understand and respond with genuine sympathy to people who are suffering—from the devastated population of Oklahoma City after the Alfred P. Murrah Building bombing to a distraught woman standing in the wreckage of a tornado in Florida—and to offer hope without denying the seriousness of loss.

Most commentators, however, while acknowledging the moral value of Clinton's always-fitting gestures of sympathy—the comfort they give, the healing they aid—generally assign such acts little importance in an overall judgment of his presidency. "He's good at funerals," a friend remarked dismissively. But there is deeper, unnoticed importance to a well-developed capacity for empathy in a leader. And that is the value of empathy as a sense of connection among the people of a society, a grasp that we share in the contingencies of the human condition amid the pressures of our historical times.

For a leader to exemplify values that connect a country's people in a basic way, in spite of their differences, is important in any political system. But the quality of empathy has particular importance, crucial importance for an inclusive politics—and not just as a quality of leadership. It is important to a sense of connection among the people generally, to their willingness to do the talking and listening necessary to lay the groundwork for generous social policies—and their willingness to pay for them.

I would emphasize that, in talking about empathy, I do not mean a generalized altruistic commitment to the well-being of all humanity. I do not mean a state of selfless moral purity. I do not think that entire populations, or even many individuals, can attain a constant, passionate concern for people beyond a close circle of family and friends. To try to base a political system on an assumption of widespread altruism in a society would be futile.

But empathy is something else. It is an emotional understanding of trouble and suffering and an identification with it. It is the basis for a desire to help. But to become strong enough to sustain a new politics of social responsibility, it has to be nurtured, respected, and supported as a core value and practice. This is why empathy in a leader is important and why the empathy that Bill Clinton consistently demonstrates is important. It signals the possibility of a deeper democracy than we have now. It supplies another piece of a rough model for the future.

Then finally there is a quality in Bill Clinton's leadership that is perhaps most important of all. Novelist James Carroll, recalling Clinton's childhood in a troubled, sometimes violent, home, described him—admiringly—as "a fractured person who is doing his best."[9] Fractured may be too strong a word to describe Clinton's makeup. Wounded might be better, certainly ill-disciplined, sexually irresponsible. But in spite of faults and flaws, he has always thrown himself into the work of politics and government with phenomenal energy and spirit. The day after reports of the Lewinsky affair surfaced in January 1998, he marched into the Congress, smiling, head high, and delivered a powerful State of the Union message—and he did it again in 1999 in the midst of his impeachment trial in the Senate.

His example of overcoming adversity, picking himself up and going on, is important as a reiteration of the American spirit of self-confidence, the belief that it is always possible to rise above bad fortune, to overcome obstacles, to defy the strictures of fate. But in the Clinton example, these classic American messages come with a different and highly significant twist.

In truly classic form, the messages are based on the Enlightenment premise of natural order in the society, a harmony of essential interests, a natural logic in social institutions—markets, families—that provide a foundation for boundless individual enterprise. Throughout the country's history, American optimism and energy could flow freely in the belief that there were no deep fractures in the society—only wrongs that could easily be put right.

What Clinton exemplifies is an outpouring of optimism and energy in the knowledge of weakness, wounds, and sorrow—frailties in the self and in the society. Of course, the frailties, the disharmonies, unbalance, and conflict were always there. But we couldn't name them in all of their complication and act on them politically. Now, signs of deep, unresolved troubles—a national deficit of care, persistent inequalities for women and minorities, persistent poverty—have pushed themselves to the political surface. The old beliefs in a firm natural order are no longer sustainable. We need new common understandings, an acceptance of inevitable conflict as a constant part of our lives. We need a Clintonesque knowledge of deep fractures combined with ebullient determination to keep going, keep trying.

Where, then, does Clinton's ill-fated Oval Office affair and the ensuing demands for his removal from office fit in this roster of new leadership virtues? I think they fit at the heart of the matter. That is, I see the extraordinary heat of the political battle provoked by the sex scandal as—in important part—a reaction to the kind of leader Clinton was.

In literary terms, the arc of the Clinton presidency follows the lines of classical tragedy: a king, a leader, a hero falls (or, in Clinton's case, almost falls) from high station because of a tragic flaw.

Clinton's personal flaw, of course, was an out-of-bounds sexual appetite and disregard for its consequences—to the women he seduces, to his family, to the offices he holds, to the people he serves. But at a deeper level, the fatal flaw in this story is that Bill Clinton was not a hero in the sense that tradition has required of American presidents. He had departed significantly from that tradition, and in doing so, he had provoked the furies of enemies who believed that he had stolen the hero's place. The pitched battle over Clinton's fitness for office was, beneath the surface, a battle over what a president should be, a fight waged by traditionalists seeking to keep the warrior-hero virtues—and functions—in place.

This is a battle that began in the '60s in the New Left uprising against established authority and all the cultural rules intertwined with it. There were, of course, the war protests, joined by the young Bill Clinton. There were the Great Society programs, seeking to harness the power of government to rewrite the social contract—to empower blacks, women, and the poor. There was the Legal Services Corporation, long served by Hillary Clinton and a band of poverty lawyers seeking to build new walls of protection for the powerless against corporations, landlords, police, and the judiciary itself. In universities students and young faculty relentlessly questioned old understandings of history, of literature, of all the old disciplines. They denied fixed truths as set down by established authorities, insisting on multiple and relative meanings, even of language itself. Women's consciousness-raising groups began serious questioning of the old rules of marriage and of the gendered division of labor. And then there was the sexual revolution that threw all the old conceptions of right and wrong relations between the sexes into confusion. Power in the society was shifting.

But the establishments fought back, to protect their prerogatives and their conceptions of the way things should be. They had the backing, for a while, of lower- and middle-class workers whose security was disrupted by economic and cultural change. Then Richard Nixon, the first beneficiary of this reaction, overreached. He was a warrior-hero president in a literal sense, uninterested in domestic issues, focused on foreign threats to the nation, endlessly interpreting their nuances. He played the role of the protector. And he abused the powers of the presidency to defeat his political enemies and to stay in office.

The mistrust of power, of established institutions, of the cold war–empowered presidency—all of the mistrust that had fed the '60s rebellions—coalesced in the political consensus that forced Nixon out of office. It also produced the Special Prosecutor's Office, designed by the Congress to limit the power of the presidency by subjecting administrative officials to investigations that the president could not control. The warrior-hero, the supposed protector against wrongdoing, was himself coming under increased suspicion as a potential wrongdoer.

Even Ronald Reagan, a textbook hero-president, came under prosecutorial scrutiny for secret violations of a congressional ban on aid to the right-wing "contra" guerrillas seeking to overthrow the leftist government of Nicaragua. Reagan survived in office, however, *because* of his heroic qualities. That is, in his campaign to deregulate business, to devolve federal functions to the states, to defund the left generally, he was using the powers of the presidency, as the warrior-hero is supposed to do, to protect the country's private systems against what they regard as harm. He was vigilantly protecting the old order and the old order was protecting him. George Bush followed in this tradition.

Then Bill Clinton entered the scene, bringing the '60s challenges to the established order back into the picture—in his generation, in his persona, and in his politics. Suddenly the corporate world, the military, the country's religions and elders were faced with a war-protesting, saxophone-playing, doughnut-eating, smiling, chatting, philandering political genius who proposed to overhaul and drastically regulate the entire health care industry—with the help of his lawyer-wife. And while he was at it, he would admit gays to the military and women and blacks to high office, and hand out condoms to teenagers in the schools.

So the protectors of the old economic and social order went on the attack. A Republican-sponsored organization called Citizens United began to provide the media with tips on an old Arkansas financial scandal, the now famous Whitewater land deal involving the Clintons. By early 1994, just a year after Clinton took office, a special prosecutor had been appointed to examine possible crimes in the Clintons' connections to Whitewater. Within six months, that appointee had been replaced—at the behest of the conservative Republican judge heading the panel in charge of prosecutorial appointments—by Kenneth Starr, another conservative. Starr then proceeded to delve into every aspect of the Clintons' public and private lives, as well as those of their associates, from Arkansas days straight through the Clinton presidency. And after the 1994 elections, the now Republican-controlled Congress carried on continual investigations of Whitewater and a succession of claimed abuses of power by the Clinton White House until the legal bills of the Clintons and other officials were in the millions.

By 1998, after four years of investigation, Whitewater and related matters had yielded no criminal charges against the Clintons. And political attacks on Bill Clinton as an advocate of big spending by big government had been largely deflected by his retreat from liberal causes, particularly in his acceptance of the 1996 welfare law and a balanced federal budget allowing virtually no new social spending.

But, unappeased by this conversion, conservatives persisted in their battle until Starr—backed by Paula Jones's lawyers, themselves backed by the wealthy, conservative Rutherford Institute—hit pay dirt with sex. Here was a legacy of the '60s that remained disturbing across political lines. The problem of defining right and wrong sexual behavior had been nowhere near resolved in a country still heavily influenced by its Puritan heritage. Recall that Joycelyn Elders had been run out of office for uttering the word "masturbation" once—at a United Nations meeting of physicians and public health officials. Now Americans were reading in the morning papers and hearing on the nightly news about oral sex, phone sex, and the touching of breasts, buttocks, and genitalia, maybe through clothing, maybe not. And congressional Republicans, hoping that embarrassing images of presidential license would provoke popular outrage at Clinton, as well as demands for his removal from office, made public more and more salacious details.

But, as we've seen, their effort backfired as polls revealed that a large majority of Americans, while disapproving of Clinton's conduct, did not regard it as grounds for impeachment. This was evidence of cultural change that horrified conservatives but allowed congressional Democrats to block the president's removal from office.

More significant yet, however, was a consistently high level of public approval of Bill Clinton's leadership. Most often attributed to his stewardship of a strong economy, that support reflected also at least tacit acceptance of a new presidential style.

Bill Clinton was a leader operating between two political eras—one in which it seemed that the business of America was business, that the country could run itself if the government simply enforced the rules of the game; and one in which it was becoming apparent that the welfare of the people required some conscious public design. The earlier era called for warrior-hero leaders, the later one for . . . something else, something postheroic.

We need to develop further a postheroic mode of leadership. It is crucial to a politics of care, a politics of equality, a politics of public well-being. And the key is to widen the reach of real democracy, to widen the political conversation, to invent channels of political discussion that bring multiple perspectives to bear on important questions and choices. Paradoxically, Bill Clinton's hounding nemesis, the Special Prosecutor's Office, was intended as a democratizing tool—but only in a negative sense, to guard against undemocratic abuse. We need to construct positive democratic processes that provide a two-way flow of thought and information between leaders and people in their communities, processes not dependent on the interests, whims, and hysterias of the media.

Whatever else Bill Clinton's presidency may come to mean in the aftermath of a sex scandal and impeachment, he has offered the country a sketch of what a new democratically inclusive mode of leadership might look like—open-ended, talking, listening, empathetic, realistic but hopeful. And yet it is only a sketch, not a fully formed model. Clinton is a transitional figure, breaking out of old forms while still compelled to function in them. He stands in the odd position of prefiguring a new politics for which the groundwork has not yet been built.

This strange disjunction is nowhere clearer than in Clinton's early so-called town meetings, televised exchanges of questions and answers between the president and selected audiences. These were gestures symbolically recognizing the value of public participation in policy discussions, but they were not real conversations. The people involved were not engaged in discussion with each other, especially not the television audience at home. There was no conversational system through which they could deepen their own information and understanding as a basis for positions they might want to advocate.

Further, the presidential office was to some degree in control of the meetings, from the selection of the audience to the selection of camera shots—which faces, which reactions. The point was less for the people to inform the president than for the president to present himself, his views and his personality, to the people.[10]

The salient point, however, is not that Bill Clinton was engaged in a phantom dialogue. It is that no real dialogue could take place because the people were not organized to engage in one. There were no clear, open, democratic channels to bring a range of voices to places of leadership. Bill Clinton was practicing a politics that did not yet exist.

Now we need to invent it.

CHAPTER 10

A NEW POLITICS OF
CONVERSATION

How do we invent a new politics of inclusion, a way of bringing into real political dialogue all of the American constituencies with all of their starkly differing interests? What is the model? How would it work? And could it work in a country this large, this diverse, this distracted by unending consumer options, this full of power surges, of immense wealth unequally distributed, this habituated to individual choices and private decision-making?

My answer to the last question is that a new politics *is* possible because the need is great. We have stress and trouble intruding into families of all kinds, at all income levels. Our present politics cannot locate the underlying problems, and people are becoming seriously alienated from political life as they know it. Only about 50 percent of those eligible voted for president in 1992 and 1996, and this was markedly higher than the shocking 39 percent who turned out for the congressional elections in 1994.

The system is not working well, and the restless energy of Americans will push and press at this dilemma until something gives. In fact we have already seen substantial reform movements mounted throughout the country. Most, however, have not grasped the deep source of trouble. Rather, relying on the usual wrongdoer-focused assumptions, they have identified the problem to be solved as the behavior of wrongdoer politicians—remote, self-concerned office holders who are destroying the connection between citizen and government.

This view is most obvious at the pathological extremes where disaffected groups see government as not just out of touch, inefficient, or corrupt but as an outright enemy, a deliberate, dangerous betrayer of the people's interest. Their responses range from efforts to expose the secret malevolence of politicians—recall allegations that White House lawyer Vincent Foster did not commit suicide but was murdered at the behest of the Clintons—to violent attacks on government, such as the 1995 Oklahoma City bombing.[1]

Mainstream responses to the disconnect between people and politicians are, of course, more tempered, aimed not at destruction but at repair. One approach is to tie elected officials more closely to voters through such mechanisms as term limits. Another is to bypass the politician altogether with direct citizen control exercised through referenda, now proliferating on state and local ballots, or through constitutional amendments.

Ross Perot, running for president in 1992, made enhanced citizen control of policy part of his campaign with a plan for *national* referenda via the Internet. In this scheme, experts would analyze a policy question and outline alternative positions; then a great citizen legislature would register its choice electronically.

Former Tennessee governor Lamar Alexander, seeking the Republican presidential nomination in 1996, had a simpler suggestion: limit legislative sessions to a few months a year, then send everybody home. In other words, eliminate politician-controlled public policy by eliminating politicians *and* public policy. Other conservatives propose extensive privatizing of governmental functions—from schooling to running prisons. Here is the American political script in pure form: there is no need for ongoing governmental guidance; the country runs itself best through its private institutions—mainly the market.

The most serious responses to perceptions of political wrongdoing are those focusing on the money problem in election campaigns. As journalist and social critic William Greider has eloquently demonstrated, and as the aftermath of the 1996 presidential election depressingly confirmed, ordinary citizens *are* cut off from their representatives by the deluge of heavy campaign contributions from favor-seeking corporations and interest groups. Clearly, where there *is* abuse of political power, reform focused on the abuse is necessary.[2]

But the general implication of these various movements, that the control or removal of wrongdoing is *all* that is necessary, is mistaken. That is where the wrongdoer analysis short-circuits well-intentioned efforts. We simply don't reach the real source of real trouble. The point is that the most serious failure with our current system does not lie in a cutoff between citizen and politician but in a cutoff among citizen, politician, *and problem.* Government is not working well, and people lose faith in politics because we do not allow ourselves to see the whole, wide complexity of social problems as political. We nibble at the edges of our large problems, such as the dual demands of family care and women's equality, and these marginal efforts can be nothing but ineffectual and further disillusioning. The first step, then, toward a real politics is to avoid false reforms, the promise of easy, one-step transformations based on the assumption that corruption or self-seeking is all we have to worry about.

The next step is to recognize that our present institutions cannot take the full measure of our present problems because they cannot register clearly enough the voices, perspectives, needs, and pressures of a wide enough range of people.

We have a variety of processes that are supposed to connect the people to policy-making—the vote; letters, petitions, testimony to committees or commissions; legislative lobbying; rallies, marches, street demonstrations; public protests, including civil disobedience—and campaign contributions. Add to these, more recently, opinion polling.

Even taken together, however, these connections do not convey to policy makers the full picture of social complexity. We've seen, in Lani Guinier's arguments, that voting, as presently organized in single-member districts, mutes minority or less powerful voices. Opinion polling can capture a wide range of views but tends to present only unconsidered, often uninformed, casual or careless reactions that do not reflect what the same people might say with more information and more thought. Furthermore, polling divides complex social issues into small slices and necessarily transmits simplified messages to officialdom. Demonstrations and protests may also send messages from the powerless, and sometimes with great effect—witness the civil rights movement in the South that defeated the rule of segregation. But generally protest movements must focus on a single issue and concentrate on removing a substantial, widely agreed upon wrong. They cannot construct solutions to complicated problems such as poverty or the country's collapsing care system.

Then there is the matter of petitioning, testifying, and lobbying—the conveying of opinions, information, interests, and ideas to governmental policy makers. Theoretically, anyone can send messages of any kind to officials. But obviously, the most powerful messages are those of huge campaign contributors—tobacco companies, communications giants, and so forth. And even apart from the factor of money, the band of voices actually using the information channels is narrow—made up largely of various policy elites, experts, consultants, and permanent lobbyists representing highly organized, if not wealthy, groups.

A substantial study of civic participation by political scientists Sidney Verba, Kay Lehman Schlozman, and Henry E. Brady demonstrates beyond question that the voices of middle- and lower-income groups are largely missing from the public conversation. "Over and over our data showed," they said, explicating extensive survey research, "that participatory input is tilted in the direction of the more advantaged groups in society—especially in terms of economic and educational position, but in terms of race and ethnicity as well." They stress both the lack of training and practice in self-representation among less privileged people as an important reason for their silence. And they also report a certain cynicism or fatalism, a belief that only money talks and that there is no point in political participation without it.[3]

The deeply serious problem for real democracy, and for the specific possibility of constructing a new politics of family care, is that elites—no matter how well intentioned—cannot fully represent the real-life situations, ideas, and priorities of people living with little money or personal power. In fact, the chronic danger is that people with power to shape policy for others will assign to those unknown others identities, characteristics, and motives that do not correspond to reality.

As the book critic Katherine Powers remarked, discussing common views of social outsiders, "As individuals they either become delineated by one trait, flattened to one dimension against the pressure of public assessment, or are granted a personality only within the confines of their particular subcultures."[4] And in Lisa Dodson's study, noted earlier, it is graphically clear that the lived experience of poverty differs radically from the terminology that describes it in public policies designed for the poor. The term "welfare mother" alone flattens a great variety of lives into one identity with strong negative judgments attached to it. The title of Dodson's book, *Don't Call Us Out of Name,* quotes the words of a woman crying out against such public misrepresentation.

Policy-making, Dodson concludes, must involve the people the policies affect. "Before the policy priorities are determined, before the reforms, investments, and programs are agreed upon, the people who will live with the policy consequences must be at the table. And they must be there from the beginning, not brought in for the photographers after all the decisions are made."[5]

A further step toward real political reform must be to add to the present system new layers of conversation that start well before official policy makers work out detailed plans. These would be conversations that start before people enter the voting booth to choose representatives who will work with experts to design policy. They would be conversations that provide the raw material for a real politics—a politics capable of identifying the real range of need, ideas, and opinions that should be the stuff of election campaigns and legislative debates.

Among political theorists, the form of politics I am conjuring up has been variously called participatory democracy, deliberative democracy, or communicative democracy. Benjamin Barber, who uses the phrase "strong democracy," describes the participatory idea as the active and continual involvement of citizens, from the grass roots to the top, in discussion and decisions about public policy—for the purpose of creating, inventing "common grounds for common living."[6]

This last point is what distinguishes the participatory concept from reforms that simply aim to tie elected officials closely to the will of those who elect them. There is no substantive purpose implicit in the close-tie reforms. Rather, they invite understandings of politics precisely as a process of bargaining to promote particular interests—a process that produces, at best, benign but incoherent results, and at worst, payoffs to the powerful. Interest group politics is not a process that can define society-wide problems, such as the caretaking crisis. It cannot express common values by responding to problems in ways that take the needs of the less powerful, or the long-range good of the society, into account.

The hope of broad participation that brings everyone to the table is that citizens across the country would gain a broad understanding of complicated social dilemmas. With respect to the care crisis, the hope is that a wide range of disparate groups talking—*to each other*—would create a composite picture showing that the crisis affects everyone, although in different ways. And such a picture could produce broad-based support for policies that take those differences into account. Such composite policies would be like those produced by interest group politics in that they would respond deliberately to a collection of disparate interests. But they would differ in that the composition would be shaped by mutual understandings of the whole.

How, then, might it be possible to get all parties to a table where they can be heard? Many people in universities and at the grass roots are trying to answer that question, and some are trying to put participatory theory into practice in various ways around the country.

In Boston, the Ways and Means Committee of the Massachusetts Senate conducted an evening budget hearing, in April 1998, in Roxbury—a section of the city in which residents are largely poor and largely black. People making up a standing-room-only crowd spoke to committee members for four hours, discussing home health care, affordable housing, salary increases for human service providers, and complications in welfare programs for victims of domestic violence.

In all probability, few of these testifiers would have been able to attend the usual daytime hearings at the State House downtown. Few would probably have felt that anyone at the State House would listen to them, in any case. Moving an official hearing to a poor city neighborhood told the residents, in effect, "We *want* to hear from you." And the residents spoke. It's a practice that could be generalized without much difficulty.[7]

The Jefferson Center for New Democratic Processes in Minnesota does generalize a practice of gathering citizens' views on local and state issues, albeit unofficially. The center organizes "policy juries" made up of a cross section of people, usually in groups of twelve, to consider specific policy proposals or problems. Their purpose is to discuss issues in depth on the basis of information provided to them, and to arrive at policy recommendations reflecting the informed judgment of ordinary citizens. They are acting, in effect, as nonauthoritative citizen legislatures—presumably providing sensible, objective opinions on questions facing their communities.

Political scientist James Fishkin advocates a similar device, which he calls "deliberative opinion polls," as a means of providing elected officials with public views that are informed and thoughtful, as opposed to the unconsidered reactions gathered by usual polling techniques.

During the 1996 election campaign, the Public Broadcasting Company, along with the University of Texas and the Presidential Libraries, put Fishkin's theory into practice in the National Issues Convention. They brought together 459 randomly selected people from around the country to study and debate campaign issues in Austin, Texas, for three days in January. What emerged, among people with widely disparate political positions, were significantly deepened and changed opinions on many controversial issues—not agreement but nuanced views. This, for Professor Fishkin, represented the true voice of the people—what people would think about issues, what they would understand about others with different interests and views, if they could personally engage in serious discussion. And the entire effort, if generalized and carried on regularly, he thought, was a means of democratizing public debate, carrying a wide medley of voices into the legislative process.[8]

All of these mechanisms are useful for the engagement of the citizenry in political affairs. But for a real democratizing of American politics to occur, *ongoing* creative conversations about social issues need to take place. And they need to involve people with widely different interests, perspectives, and agendas. Imagining how this might work, adapting present ideas for a participatory politics, inventing new procedures, designing new forums, and advocating their adoption is another task for the liberal enterprise.

Such a project of invention could take many forms. But its guiding purpose should go beyond providing policy makers with objective advice, as the Minnesota policy juries do, or providing legislators a reading of informed public opinion, as in the Fishkin design. The purpose of new forms of public deliberation should not be to meld a variety of voices into consensus, however well considered. It should be more the

opposite—to ensure that, before consensus is reached, everyone understands the degree of real conflict at hand, and how various resolutions
of that conflict would affect the most vulnerable groups involved. It
should be a process that actively elicits descriptions of the way things
are and ideas about the way things should be from people actually living with whatever situation is under discussion.

Without question, designing such a process would be an extraordinarily difficult project, which I will not attempt here. It must be, in fact,
the work of many people, many groups, talking and arguing, experimenting with pilot programs, and slowly expanding the enterprise.
Then somewhere along the line voters would have to decide, perhaps
through referenda, perhaps through their representatives, how to attach a new level of discussion to the policy-making process, how to
make it a wholly legitimate part of democratic governance.

All I propose to do at this point is to sketch some rough outlines of
issues that are sure to arise and to offer some thoughts about them.

One is the great dilemma implicit in constructing a system the purpose of which is to be unsystematic, defining procedural rules that invite people to change the rules. This is a subject that has been
painstakingly elaborated by Harvard law professor and social activist
Lucie White. She describes, for example, the paradox of the Head Start
program, which, from its beginnings in the Great Society attempts to
empower the poor, has mandated the close involvement of low-income
parents in its on-the-ground operations. They are supposed to be co-
participants in the making of policy that governs the education of their
children. But, White says, the procedures that are supposed to accomplish this result can, in practice, undermine it.

Specifically, Head Start regulations define the kinds of issues parents
are to decide, and require that meetings follow Robert's Rules of
Order, and White shows, by a detailed account of one parents' meeting, how constrained the resulting conversation can be. In this meeting, no large questions are raised; no out-of-order perspectives are
invited or described.

Another problem White identifies is the tendency of poorly educated people to defer to anyone who is or seems to be authoritative,
and to remain silent. Here, too, the program's regulations are monitory,
spelling out the need for administrators and professional staff "to avoid

dominating meetings by force of their greater training and experience." And yet, no doubt unintentionally in many instances, it happens.

The moral of the story is the need for planners of a participatory politics to be highly aware of their primary purpose, which is to open conversation and to keep it open, not to subject it to overcontrol. For example, Roberts Rules are designed to channel discussion toward votes and should probably not come into play, if at all, until open-ended discussion has identified choices to be made.[9]

Yet another large question facing organizers of such a politics is the matter of representation. To dig into the defining details of pressing social questions, some of the new conversations, if not all, should focus on particular issues. And such conversations should involve the whole array of groups for whom the issue is important. But how is it possible to decide what the relevant groups are before wide-ranging discussions have identified the major elements of the issue? The key would be great care in opening discussions of particular issues to people with a great variety of perspectives, not predeciding and preselecting the interests to be heard—black, white, rich, poor, and so forth. For example, discussions of family care and its linkage to women's equality might initially include working parents of young children, corporate CEOs, small-business managers, day-care and nursing-home owners and workers, mothers who are poor, mothers who are law firm partners, middle-class mothers taking care of children at home, middle-class mothers with part-time or full-time paid jobs, the same array of fathers, daughters taking care of elderly parents, teachers, police, and family court judges. But ensuing conversations might identify others who should be heard.[10]

I would add here a particular cautionary note about the complicated fact that many people hold multiple interests that do not fit into neat pigeonholes. To take a clear example, a black woman must generally deal with disadvantages stemming from both race and gender. At some points, perhaps in a predominantly white workplace, she might be primarily concerned with the problem of racial discrimination. At others, perhaps in finding time for her family, she would have a problem shared with women of all colors. And there are always class issues at play. A poorly educated black single mother working at a minimum-wage job and a professionally employed black woman might both face problems of racial discrimination at work and too little time at home, but the particularities of their problems would differ greatly. A participatory politics must avoid stereotypical conceptions of interest and allow people themselves to define the nature of their complicated concerns.

Then there is the problem of potential danger in the participatory enterprise, the possibility that bringing conflicting interests into the open could exacerbate misunderstanding and inflame hostilities. The need, obviously, is for people organizing the new conversations to proceed cautiously. They must set up discussions in such a way that people with strongly opposed views are able to listen to one another, to feel the full weight of the needs and convictions of others. Fortunately, there is a growing body of expertise in public dialogue to draw on. In addition to established techniques developed by professional mediators and negotiators, there are newer conversational methods being devised by groups concerned specifically with contentious public issues.

Founders of the Public Conversations Project, based in Watertown, Massachusetts, for example, have worked over the past ten years to create settings for dialogue, as opposed to debate, on difficult issues. They describe these settings as "contexts in which opponents in long-standing conflicts over public issues can move beyond stereotyping, polarizing rhetoric, and defensive reactivity, contexts where they can relate in ways that enable them to understand more fully beliefs, meaning, values, and fears held not only by their opponents, but also by themselves."

One approach used by the Public Conversations Project, and increasingly by others, is to encourage participants to describe their personal experience with the issue at hand, because "these stories steer the group away from the narrow path of polarized principles, policies, or positions." As PCP director Laura Chasin explains further, "Asking people to situate their views in their life experiences fosters attentive, thoughtful, empathic listening and encourages people who may have been known to each other only as slogan bearers to present their thoughts and feelings in a complex and multidimensional manner."[11]

Political theorist Kathleen Jones suggests that coming face-to-face with the complexity revealed by such group discussions could induce in participants a healthy humility in approaching policy questions.

They could see more easily than from the vantage point of think tanks that policy-making is a risky business, that with the best intentions you might not get things right. This perception, Jones thinks, could alter the very nature of political speech. People might be less likely to pronounce authoritatively on public issues, to express grandiose certainties and definitive judgments. More acceptable language might well be marked by hesitance, open-endedness, questioning, and listening, thus countering the risks of a verbal war of all against all.[12]

In any case, well-organized, inclusive, deliberative public conversations might actually end in agreement about specific policy proposals, but that purpose alone should not drive the discussion because it could squelch the full exploration of complicated problems. The conversations would be successful only if they clearly delineated lines of difference and conflict among the groups involved, since clarity about those lines could enhance honest policy-making. It could put pressure on officials to make realistic assessments of costs and losses that follow from different policy choices—to make clear who wins and who loses in any given choice.

Just how the connection between deliberative groups and elected officials would work is a question for organizational planners. In general, it is clear enough that reports from the groups should be public. They should go to the governmental agencies and committees that deal with the issues involved. They should go to the media, to think tanks, foundations, and universities. They should go to candidates running for office. They should go to corporate boards and to unions.

But providing a flow of information and opinion to decision makers would not be the only benefit of new deliberative conversations. Because they would bring together people in widely differing social situations to discuss an issue that affects them all, the conversations could provide the basis for the formation of new political coalitions. That is, clusters of participants with differing positions could find that, with increased knowledge and insight about one another, they could work together on specific points to advocate specific policies.

What such conversations could mean for women dealing in their multiple ways with the intertwined questions of care and equality is the possibility of sorting out their differences and commonalities. With face-to-face contact and mutual understanding, they could recognize and discuss what care problems looked like from their different economic, cultural, and ideological positions. And they could also see that they shared problems of time for families, of unequal opportunities in workplaces at all levels, of unequal responsibilities at home, and also worries about sexual harassment, rape, and other threats of violence. With these deepened understandings, they could form cross-class, cross-race coalitions to work out packages of agreed-upon policies. Some, such as nonpunitive welfare requirements, might be designed to respond to the needs of one group of women; others, such as restructured work time, might be a common concern. But whatever the agenda, its support from a coalition greatly increases its chances of success.

A participatory politics that actually worked would be enormously demanding of the citizenry. Who would participate? Who would be willing to? Who would have the time? The last question is the easiest. Time could be subsidized—perhaps through public-private collaborations. But willingness would depend on the desire of American citizens to sustain a healthy society.

I think the desire is strong. I think that new connections established between people and government, connections that allow people to keep sight of common purposes while being open about their differences, could release new civic energy. With real democracy a possibility, we could see a new willing engagement in real politics and a new stage in the American experiment.

NOTES

Prologue

1. Knopf, 1986.

Chapter 1

1. *Women Lawyers—Rewriting the Rules,* New York: Plume/Penguin, 1995.

Chapter 2

1. *New York Times,* May 14, 1994, p. 10.
2. Boston: Little Brown, 1996.
3. See James A. Morone, "The Corrosive Politics of Virtue," in *The American Prospect,* May–June 1996, p. 30, for a strong critique of the focus on wrongdoing in present politics and its undermining of liberal strength.
4. Kathleen E. Christensen, "Contingent Work Arrangements in Family-Sensitive Corporations in the United States," in *Perspectives on Employment Stability,* Cambridge, MA: Radcliffe Public Policy Institute, 1996, pp. 33–52.
5. The four-state study: Susan Chira, "Care at Child Day Centers is Rated as Poor," *New York Times,* February 7, 1995, p. A12; the Families and Work Institute study: Tamar Lewin, "Fewer Children per Care Provider Is Good for All, Study Finds," *New York Times,* March 7, 1998, p. A6.
6. Debra West, "When the Quest for Child Care Leads Home," *New York Times,* August 17, 1997, Section 3, p. 13.
7. Ellen Galinsky, Carollee Lowes, Susan Kontos, and Marybeth Shinn, *The Study of Children in Family Child Care and Relative Care,* New York: Families and Work Institute, 1994. For a review of other studies supporting the same discouraging conclusions, see Diane Eyer, *Mother Guilt: How Our Culture Blames Mothers for What's Wrong with Society,* New York: Times Books, 1996.

8. *Don't Call Us Out of Name: The Untold Lives of Women and Girls in Poor America,* Boston: Beacon Press, 1998, p. 215.

9. "Facts on Working Women," United States Department of Labor, Women's Bureau, no. 98, May 1, 1998, p. 2.

10. For a detailed picture of the social context behind my neighbor's story, see Emily K. Abel, *Who Cares for the Elderly? Public Policy and the Experiences of Adult Daughters,* Philadelphia: Temple University Press, 1991. For specific kinds of public support that family caretakers need, see also Abel's chapter "Family Care of the Frail Elderly," in Emily K. Abel and Margaret K. Nelson, eds., *Circles of Care: Work and Identity in Women's Lives,* Albany, NY: SUNY Press, 1990. For a wise discussion of the need to base paid home caregiving on measures of human need as opposed to strict efficiency, see Deborah Stone, "Care and Trembling," *The American Prospect,* March–April 1999, p. 61. And for an unsparing description of what home care for the physical needs of the seriously ill can mean, see Marion Deutsche Cohen, *Dirty Details: The Days and Nights of a Well Spouse,* Philadelphia: Temple University Press, 1996.

11. The National Assessment of Educational Progress (NEAP) report for 1994 found 40 percent of fourth graders nationwide reading at the "below-basic" or semiliterate level.

12. *Boston Globe,* June 7, 1994, p. 66.

13. *Boston Globe,* September 23, 1996, p. B1.

14. Kate Zernike, "Bad Behavior, Special Treatment," May 31, 1997, pp. A1, 8.

15. Urbana, IL: University of Illinois Press, 1994.

16. Show no. 5759, February 6, 1997. Transcript by "Strictly Business," Overland Park, Kansas.

17. *Tragedies of Our Own Making,* cited above, pp. 74–75, 135.

Chapter 3

1. *Embattled Paradise: The American Family in an Age of Uncertainty,* New York: Basic Books, pp. 196–197.

2. Faux, *The Party's Not Over: A New Vision for Democrats,* New York: Basic Books, 1996; Parker, "Centrism, Populist Style," *The Nation,* October 7, 1996, p. 19.

3. Morris, whatever his highly publicized faults—megalomania prominent among them—produced an illuminating account of the 1996 campaign in *Behind the Oval Office: Winning the Presidency in the Nineties,* New York: Random House, 1997.

4. "Work, Kids and Families," *Washington Post,* September 24, 1996, p. A18.

5. "The Protean President," *The Atlantic Monthly,* May 1996, p. 42.

6. Francis X. Clines, "A Religious Tilt toward the Left," *New York Times,* September 16, 1996, pp. A1, B8.

7. An excellent report, "Financing Child Care in the United States: An Illustrative Catalog of Current Strategies," published in 1997 by the Ewing Marion Kauffman Foundation and the Pew Charitable Trusts, records this difficulty as it examines the allocation of public general revenue for child care. In order to justify increases in child-care programs, the report states, public agencies tend to invoke rationales such as improving school readiness, preventing crime and violence, or augmenting welfare reform. That is, they do not support their proposals by referring to a general social responsibility for good care because no such principle has yet taken firm hold in the United States.

8. Tronto offers a powerful argument for the recognition of care as a basic element of political morality in *Moral Boundaries: A Political Argument for an Ethic of Care,* New York: Routledge, 1993. For a strong analysis of the public importance of valuing care, see also Michele M. Moody-Adams, "The Social Construction and Reconstruction of Care," in David M. Estlund and Martha C. Nussbaum, eds., *Sex, Preference, and Family: Essays on Law and Nature,* New York: Oxford University Press, 1997, p. 3.

9. Marjorie L. DeVault, *Feeding the Family: The Social Organization of Caring as a Gendered Work,* Chicago: University of Chicago Press, 1991, p. 241.

10. *Who Pays for the Kids? Gender and the Structures of Constraint,* New York: Routledge, 1994, p. 95.

11. *Upton vs. JWP Businessland,* 425 Mass. 756 (Mass. 1997). Although the Upton case was based on a public policy claim, I have argued that conflicts between work hours and family care, as they are conflicts that generally affect women, should be regarded as sex discrimination in the workplace, and that civil rights lawyers should pursue this point. Mona Harrington, "Is Time-Out for Family Unprofessional?" *Trial,* February 1997, p. 70. The primary forum for the issue, however, is the political center stage.

12. *The Time Bind: When Work Becomes Home and Home Becomes Work,* New York: Metropolitan Books, 1997.

13. Bailyn's basic theory appears in *Breaking the Mold: Women, Men, and Time in the New Corporate World,* New York: Free Press, 1993. Reports on the corporate projects appear in Lotte Bailyn, Rhona Rapoport, Deborah Kolb, Joyce Fletcher, et al., "Re-Linking Work and Family: A Catalyst for Organizational Change," MIT Sloan School of Management: Working Paper no. 3892–96, April 1996; and Rhona Rapaport and Lotte Bailyn, "Relinking Life and Work: Toward a Better Future," a report to the Ford Foundation, November 1996. For a report on the Fleet project, see Lotte Bailyn and Paula Rayman, "Building a Win-Win Agenda: Radcliffe-Fleet Work and Life Integration Project," Cambridge, MA: Radcliffe Public Policy Institute, 1998.

14. Alison Mitchell, "Clinton Prods Executives to 'Do the Right Thing,'" *New York Times,* May 17, 1996, p. D1.

15. "The Family and Medical Leave Act," Cambridge, MA: Radcliffe Public Policy Institute, 1996.

16. For highly informed and highly critical analyses of the welfare law, see commentaries by the Clinton administration officials who resigned over its passage: Mary Jo Bane, "Welfare as We Might Know It," *The American Prospect,* no. 30, January–February 1997, p. 47; Peter Edelman, "The Worst Thing Bill Clinton Has Done," *The Atlantic Monthly,* March 1997, p. 43; and Wendell E. Primus, "The Safety Net Works," *Washington Post National Weekly Edition,* October 14–20, 1996, p. 27.

17. Phelps, *Rewarding Work: How to Restore Participation and Self-Support to Free Enterprise,* Cambridge, MA: Harvard University Press, 1997, pp. 106–107; Schwarz, *Illusions of Opportunity: The American Dream in Question,* New York: Norton, 1997.

18. The Families and Work Institute study, *New York Times,* April 15, 1998, p. A18; Rubenstein, "Superdad Needs a Reality Check," op ed, *New York Times,* April 16, 1998, p. A23.

19. New York: Basic Books, 1989, p. 171.

Chapter 4

1. *The New English Bible.*
2. Sociologist Alan Wolfe in *One Nation After All: What Middle-Class Americans Really Think About God, Country, Family, Racism, Welfare, Immigration, Homosexuality, Work, the Right, the Left, and Each Other,* New York: Viking, 1998, finds in interviews with suburban families across the country a lack of strong division on social issues including those concerning families, but political debate continues to reflect sharp differences outside those relatively affluent precincts.
3. For an overview of conflicting political positions on family issues, see Janet Z. Giele, "Decline of the Family: Conservative, Liberal, and Feminist Views," in David Popenoe, Jean Bethke Elshtain, and David Blankenhorn, eds., *Promises to Keep: Decline and Renewal of Marriage in America,* Lanham, MD: Rowman and Littlefield, 1996.
4. Joycelyn Elders and David Chanoff, *Joycelyn Elders, M.D.: From Sharecropper's Daughter to Surgeon General of the United States of America,* New York: William Morrow, 1996, p. 272.
5. Hearing of the Committee on Labor and Human Resources, U.S. Senate, 103rd Congress, 1st session, on Joycelyn Elders to be Surgeon General, July 23, 1993, pp. 67, 75.
6. Elders and Chanoff, pp. 241–242, 291.
7. Quotes from the *Washington Post,* February 16, 1993, and the *Los Angeles Times,* March 8, 1993, Elders and Chanoff, p. 169.
8. Elders and Chanoff, p. 304.
9. *Boston Globe,* June 25, 1994, p. 6.
10. *New York Times,* August 1, 1994, p. A1.
11. *Boston Globe,* November 14, 1994, pp. 1, 8.
12. Elders and Chanoff, pp. 331–334.
13. Cambridge, MA: Harvard University Press, 1996, pp. 181–182.
14. In a Gallup poll asking whether adultery should be a crime in the United States, 61 percent of the respondents answered no. *New York Times,* June 9, 1997, pp. A1, 18.

Chapter 5

1. For a thorough discussion of the historical relativity of family systems, see Stephanie Coontz, *The Way We Never Were: American Families and the Nostalgia Trap,* New York: Basic Books, 1992.
2. "'Surrogate Mothering' and Women's Freedom: A Critique of Contracts for Human Reproduction," *Signs,* vol. 18, no. 3, 1993, p. 618; see also Martha Minow and Mary Lyndon Shanley, "Relational Rights and Responsibilities: Revisioning the Family in Liberal Political Theory and Law," *Hypatia,* vol. 11, no. 1, winter 1996, p. 4, and Mary Lyndon Shanley, "Unencumbered Individuals and Embedded Selves: Reasons to Resist Dichotomous Thinking in Family Law," in *Debating Democracy's Discontent,* Anita L. Allen and Milton C. Regan, Jr., eds., New York: Oxford Unversity Press, 1998, p. 229.
3. For extensive information about the lives, and detailed budgets, of single mothers on welfare throughout the country, see Kathryn Edin and Laura Lein, *Making Ends Meet: How Single Mothers Survive Welfare and Low-Wage Work,* New York: Russell Sage Foundation, 1996. For statistical demonstrations of the connection between work structures and family poverty, see Randy Albelda and Chris Tilly, *Glass Ceilings and Bottomless Pits: Women's Work, Women's Poverty,* Boston: South End Press, 1997.

4. *On Our Own: Unmarried Motherhood in America,* New York: Random House, 1997, p. 400.

5. David Blankenhorn, Steven Bayme, and Jean Bethke Elshtain, *Rebuilding the Nest: A New Commitment to the American Family,* Milwaukee, WI: Family Service America, 1990; George Feifer, *Divorce: An Oral Portrait,* New York: New Press, 1995; Maggie Gallagher, *The Abolition of Marriage,* Washington, DC: Regnery, 1996; Mary Ann Glendon, *Abortion and Divorce in Western Law: American Failures, European Challenges,* Cambridge, MA: Harvard University Press, 1987; Diane Medved with Dan Quayle, *The American Family: Discovering Values That Make Us Strong,* New York: Harper-Collins, 1996; David Popenoe, *Life without Father,* New York: Martin Kessler Books, 1996; Barbara Dafoe Whitehead, *The Divorce Culture: How Divorce Became an Entitlement and How It Is Blighting the Lives of Our Children,* New York: Knopf, 1997.

6. *New York Times,* (Christian Coalition), June 24, 1997, p. A1; (Etzioni), August 13, 1997, op ed, p. A29.

7. Skolnick, "Family Values: The Sequel," *The American Prospect,* May–June 1997, p. 86; Stacey, *In the Name of the Family: Rethinking Family Values in the Postmodern Age,* Boston: Beacon, 1996; Kurz, *For Richer, for Poorer: Mothers Confront Divorce,* New York: Routledge, 1995. See also Susan B. Apel, "Communitarianism and Feminism: The Case Against the Preference for the Two-Parent Family," in Karen J. Maschke, ed., *Reproduction, Sexuality, and the Family,* New York: Garland, 1997, p. 251.

8. "Always Our Children: A Pastoral Message to Parents of Homosexual Children and Suggestions for Pastoral Ministers," a statement of the Bishops' Committee on Marriage and Family, National Conference of Catholic Bishops, Washington, DC: United States Catholic Conference, Inc., 1997.

9. Report to the General Convention on the Blessing of Same-Sex Relationships, prepared by members of the Standing Liturgical Commission and the Theology Committee of the House of Bishops, 1997.

10. "Dispatches and Dialogues," *Slate,* www.slate.com, March 10, 1997.

11. "Since When Is Marriage a Path to Liberation?" from *OUT/LOOK National Gay and Lesbian Quarterly,* no. 6, fall 1989, included in *Same-Sex Marriage: Pro and Con, a Reader,* Andrew Sullivan, ed., New York: Vintage, 1997, pp. 118, 119, 121.

12. "Why Marry?" from the *New York Times,* April 17, 1996, included in Sullivan, *Same-Sex Marriage,* at pp. 132,133.

13. "Dispatches and Dialogues," *Slate,* www.slate.com, March 10, 1997. For the slave experience in relation to marriage and family, see Peggy Cooper Davis, *Neglected Stories: The Constitution and Family Values,* New York: Hill and Wang, 1997.

14. Susan Moller Okin makes this argument in "Sexual Orientation and Gender: Dichotomizing Differences," in David M. Estlund and Martha C. Nussbaum, eds., *Sex, Preference, and Family: Essays on Law and Nature,* New York: Oxford University Press, 1997, pp. 44, 54–56. Judith Stacey makes a similar point in *In the Name of the Family: Rethinking Family Values in the Postmodern Age,* Boston: Beacon, 1996, p. 15.

15. Alan Wolfe, in *One Nation After All,* New York: Viking, 1998, found homosexuality and particularly gay marriage to be the main exceptions to a general lack of division over social issues among his middle-class suburban interviewees.

16. "A Partnership with American Families," in Stanley B. Greenberg and Theda Skocpol, eds., *The New Majority: Toward a Popular Progressive Politics,* New Haven: Yale University Press, 1997, pp. 104, 121.

Chapter 6

1. August 1992, pp. 25–32.
2. *New York Times,* April 28, 1992, p. A19.
3. *New York Times,* Letters, October 26, 1995, p. A24.
4. *Boston Sunday Globe,* March 1, 1998, p. C1.
5. *Choosing to Lead: Women and the Crisis of American Values,* Boston: Beacon Press, 1996, pp. 32–33.
6. For the early evolution of True Womanhood, see Nancy Cott, *The Bonds of Womanhood: "Women's Sphere" in New England, 1780–1835,* New Haven, CT: Yale University Press, 1977.
7. *Choosing to Lead,* p. 18.
8. *Desires of a Woman's Heart,* Wheaton, IL: Tyndale, 1993, p. 204, quoted in Linda Kintz, *Between Jesus and the Market: The Emotions That Matter in Right-Wing America,* Durham, NC: Duke University Press, 1997, p. 38.
9. *Can Motherhood Survive? A Christian Looks at Social Parenting,* Brentwood, TN: Wolgemuth and Hyatt, 1990, p. 2, quoted in Kintz, *Between Jesus and the Market,* p. 40.
10. *New York Times,* June 10, 1998, pp. A1, A24. Quote, p. A24.
11. *Octogesima Adveniens.*
12. New York: Times Books, 1996. For criticism of excessive blame placed on mothers as the source of all pathologies, see also Shari Thurer, *The Myths of Motherhood,* Boston: Houghton Mifflin, 1994.
13. New York: New York University Press, 1997, pp. 81–82, 111.
14. New Haven, CT: Yale University Press, 1996. For a trenchant review essay on these and other books on the conflicting demands of mothering and paid work, see Deborah Stone, "Work and the Moral Woman," *The American Prospect,* November–December 1997, p. 78.
15. *Boston Globe,* May 9, 1997, p. A3.
16. The speech was given on April 6, 1993; the cover story by Michael Kelly appeared on May 23, 1993. The speech reflected the ideas of social critic Michael Lerner, who writes that his association with the Clintons ended abruptly in the wake of the severe criticism Hillary took for championing his conception of political values. See "My Time with the Clintons" in Lerner's *The Politics of Meaning: Restoring Hope and Possibility in an Age of Cynicism,* Reading, MA: Addison Wesley, 1997, pp. 310–315.
17. *Boston Globe,* January 8, 1998, p. A20.
18. *New York Times,* October 23, 1997, p. A24.
19. January 8, 1998. The essay, "A Dangerous Experiment in Child-Rearing," is by attorney Andrew Peyton Thomas.
20. *New York Times,* January 25, 1998, Section 1, p. 22.
21. *The Neutered Mother, the Sexual Family, and Other Twentieth-Century Tragedies,* New York: Routledge, 1995. But for criticism of Fineman's specific proposals, see Diane Harriford and Mary Lyndon Shanley, "Revisioning Family Law: Review Essay," *Law and Society Review,* vol. 30, no. 2, 1996, p. 437.

Chapter 7

1. For an apt analysis of these tensions, see Cynthia Enloe, "The Masculine Mystique," *The Progressive,* January 1994, p. 24, and for a wider discussion, her book *The Morning After: Sexual Politics at the End of the Cold War,* Berkeley, CA: University of Cali-

fornia Press, 1993. For highly sensitive and penetrating appraisals of the connection between masculinity and the warrior role, see also Carol Cohn's essays, including "Sex and Death in the Rational World of Defense Intellectuals," *Signs,* vol. 12, no. 4, summer 1987, p. 687; "Emasculating America's Linguistic Deterrent," in Adrienne Harris and Ynestra King, eds., *Rocking the Ship of State,* Boulder, CO: Westview, 1989; and "Wars, Wimps, and Women," in Miriam Cooke and Angela Woolacott, eds., *Gendering War Talk,* Princeton, NJ: Princeton University Press, 1993.

2. For an extended discussion of this peculiarly American conception of governing, see my book *The Dream of Deliverance in American Politics,* New York: Knopf, 1986.

3. "Of Knights and Presidents: Race of Mythic Proportions," *New York Times,* October 10, 1992, pp. 1, 9.

4. For a brilliant analysis of remaining attachments to the warrior in American society, see James William Gibson, *Warrior Dreams: Violence and Manhood in Post-Vietnam America,* New York: Hill and Wang, 1994.

5. *Boston Globe,* May 4, 1994, p. 3.

6. These quotes are from an article by Peter J. Boyer analyzing the political tensions surrounding Admiral Boorda: "Admiral Boorda's War," *The New Yorker,* September 16, 1996, pp. 68, 74. For another long article tracing this background, see Nick Kotz, "What Really Happened to Admiral Boorda," *Washingtonian,* December 1996, pp. 94–121.

7. The Kotz article, just cited, contains the text of a suicide note Boorda left for "his sailors" in which he urges them to keep alive the practice of "one-on-one leadership." Two years after Admiral Boorda's suicide, the secretary of the Navy, John H. Dalton, added to Boorda's official record a letter from Adm. Elmo R. Zumwalt Jr., chief of Naval Operations during the Vietnam War, stating categorically that Boorda had been entitled to wear the disputed insignia.

8. *United States v. Virginia,* 518 U.S. 515 (1996). The Citadel had also been embroiled in sex discrimination suits, but the VMI case reached the Supreme Court first.

9. *New York Times,* January 18, 1996, p. A18.

10. "The Warrior Besieged," *New York Times Magazine,* June 22, 1997, pp. 25, 26.

11. Foote: *New York Times,* December 12, 1997, p. A26; Donnelly, Mariner: *Boston Globe,* December 21, 1997, pp. D1, D5.

12. For a thorough explication of these questions, see Linda Bird Francke, *Ground Zero: The Gender Wars in the Military,* New York: Simon and Schuster, 1997.

13. Joe Klein, "Socket Moms," *The New Yorker,* April 13, 1998, pp. 28, 32.

14. "Where Women Are Women and So Are Men," *Harper's Magazine,* May 1998, p. 65.

Chapter 8

1. "Will Class Trump Gender?" *The American Prospect,* November–December 1996, p. 44.

2. Blair remarks in "Giving Women the Business," *Harper's Magazine,* December 1997, pp. 47–58; Crittenden, "Yes, Motherhood Lowers Pay," op-ed, *New York Times,* August 22, 1995, p. A15. More generally, see Crittenden's book, *What Our Mothers Didn't Tell Us: Why Happiness Eludes the Modern Woman,* New York: Simon and Schuster, 1999. For IWF positions on social policy, see also its journal *Women's Quarterly.*

3. *Don't Call Us Out of Name: The Untold Lives of Women and Girls in Poor America,* Boston: Beacon Press, 1998.

4. *Slouching Towards Gomorrah,* New York: HarperCollins, 1996.

5. "Giving Women the Business," roundtable discussion, *Harper's Magazine,* December 1997, pp. 47, 50.
6. The classic text on sexual harassment is Catharine A. MacKinnon, *Sexual Harassment of Working Women,* New Haven, CT: Yale University Press, 1979. See also my capsule history of the development of sexual harassment law through the *Meritor* case in *Women Lawyers—Rewriting the Rules,* New York: Plume/Penguin, 1995, pp. 210–215. And for a complete exposition of case law before and after *Meritor,* see Vicki Schultz, "Reconceptualizing Sexual Harassment," *Yale Law Journal,* vol. 107, no. 6, April 1998, p. 1683.
7. Apparently most employers that have sexual harassment policies in place do not have policies against consensual relationships—that is, romances—in the workplace. Jeffrey L. Seglin, "Between Consenting Co-Workers," *New York Times,* September 20, 1998, Section 3, p. 4.
8. Vicki Schultz, "Reconceptualizing Sexual Harassment," *Yale Law Journal,* vol. 107, no. 6, April 1998, p. 1683. Schultz's long review of the case law on sexual harassment is a particularly valuable record of precise factual examples of harassing behavior.
9. The threatened retribution case: *Burlington Industries v. Ellerth,* 118 Sup. Ct. 2257 (1998); the lewd conduct case: *Faragher v. City of Boca Raton,* 118 Sup. Ct. 2275 (1998).
10. *The War Against Parents: What We Can Do for America's Beleaguered Moms and Dads,* Boston: Houghton Mifflin, 1998, p. 95.
11. Chapter 3, "Managerial Greed and the Collapse of Economic Security," *The War Against Parents;* quote, p. 83.
12. "Relational Practice: A Feminist Reconstruction of Work," *Journal of Management Inquiry,* vol. 7, no. 2, June 1998, p. 163.
13. Lea Grundy and Netsy Firestein, "Work, Family, and the Labor Movement," Cambridge, MA: Radcliffe Public Policy Institute, 1997.

Chapter 9

1. For Lani Guinier's full account of her nomination experience and an explication of her theories of democratic representation, see *Lift Every Voice: Turning a Civil Rights Setback into a New Vision of Social Justice,* New York: Simon and Schuster, 1998. For a collection of the controversial articles that blocked her appointment to the Justice Department, see *The Tyranny of the Majority: Fundamental Fairness in Representative Democracy,* New York: Free Press, 1994.
2. *Lift Every Voice: Turning a Civil Rights Setback into a New Vision of Social Justice,* p. 302. Discussion of ideas for such change now percolating through the country follows in chapter 10.
3. June 29, 1994, p. 16.
4. "A Place Called Fear," *The New Yorker,* April 3, 1995, pp. 38, 42.
5. *New York Times,* June 16, 1994, pp. C1, 6.
6. *Leadership without Easy Answers,* Cambridge, MA: Harvard University Press, 1994, p. 118.
7. I have examined the silencing and alienation of many women law students subjected to this kind of training in *Women Lawyers—Rewriting the Rules,* New York: Plume/Penguin, 1995; and Lani Guinier, writing with Michelle Fine and Jane Balin, argues powerfully that training aggressors to do important work in the society is harmful to social health, in *Becoming Gentlemen: Women, Law School and Institutional Change,* Boston: Beacon Press, 1997.

8. *New York Times,* July 7, 1995, p. B3.

9. "Clinton's Compassion—and His Struggle," *Boston Globe,* March 3, 1998, p. A11.

10. See Robert E. Denton Jr. and Rachel L. Holloway, "Clinton and the Town Hall Meetings: Mediated Conversation and the Risk of Being 'In Touch,'" in Denton and Holloway, eds., *The Clinton Presidency: Images, Issues, and Communication Strategies,* Westport, CT: Praeger, 1996.

Chapter 10

1. For excellent analyses of right-wing political alienation, and particularly strains connected to the Vietnam War and the experience of its veterans, see James William Gibson, *Warrior Dreams: Violence and Manhood in Post-Vietnam America,* New York: Hill and Wang, 1994; and Jonathan Shay, *Achilles in Vietnam: Combat Trauma and the Undoing of Character,* New York: Simon and Schuster, 1994.

2. *Who Will Tell the People? The Betrayal of American Democracy,* New York: Simon and Schuster, 1992.

3. *Voice and Equality: Civic Voluntarism in American Politics,* Cambridge, MA: Harvard University Press, 1995, p. 512.

4. *Boston Globe,* February 5, 1995, p. 59. A review of *We Came All the Way from Cuba So You Could Dress Like That?* by Achy Obejas.

5. *Don't Call Us Out of Name: The Untold Lives of Women and Girls in Poor America,* Boston: Beacon Press, 1998, p. 220.

6. Benjamin Barber, *A Passion for Democracy,* Princeton, NJ: Princeton University Press, 1998, p. 12. The foremost theorist of deliberative democracy is the German philosopher Jürgen Habermas. He attempts, not wholly successfully, to apply his highly abstract thought to the practice of politics in *Between Facts and Norms: Contributions to a Discourse Theory of Law and Diplomacy,* William Rehg, trans., Cambridge, MA: MIT Press, 1996. For an interpretive essay on deliberative democracy generally, see Jane Mansbridge, "Feminism and Democracy," *The American Prospect,* spring 1990, p. 126.

7. *Boston Globe,* April 17, 1998, p. A20.

8. For the theory, see James S. Fishkin, *Democracy and Deliberation: New Directions for Democratic Reform,* New Haven, CT: Yale University Press, 1991. Accounts of the National Issues Convention appear in the *New York Times,* January 22, 1996, p. A13, and January 27, 1996, p. 8.

9. Lucie White, "Ordering Voice: Rhetoric and Democracy in Project Head Start," in Austin Sarat and Thomas B. Kearns, eds., *The Rhetoric of Law,* Ann Arbor: University of Michigan Press, 1996, p. 185. White's book on the Head Start experience and related issues is forthcoming. For experience with the problem of intimidation, see also Pamela Wescott, *Across the Divide,* Cambridge, MA: Radcliffe Public Policy Institute, 1997, a report on 1996 experiments with "community-based models of public policy dialogue" in Boston and Cambridge.

10. Public law professors and practitioners are giving increased attention to the problem of fair representation of all groups concerned in class action lawsuits involving multiple parties. See Susan P. Sturm, "A Normative Theory of Public Law Remedies," *Georgetown Law Journal,* vol. 79, 1991, p. 1355; and "The Promise of Participation," *Iowa Law Review,* vol. 78, no. 5, July 1993, p. 981.

11. The quotation from Laura Chasin is in a fax to the author. The other quotes are from a multiauthored article: Richard Chasin, Margaret Herzig, Sallyann Roth, Laura Chasin, Carol Becker, Robert R. Stains Jr., "From Diatribe to Dialogue on Divisive

Public Issues: Approaches Drawn from Family Therapy," *Mediation Quarterly,* vol. 13, no. 4, summer 1996, pp. 323, 324, 335. To date, the Public Conversations Project has worked primarily in off-the-record settings to encourage the maximum openness of participants. But other groups, such as the organizers of the National Issues Convention, use similar techniques in open, or quasi-open meetings.

12.   *Compassionate Authority: Democracy and the Representation of Women,* New York: Routledge, 1993.

INDEX

abortion, 64, 69, 71, 72, 82
adoption, 89, 144
adultery, 75–8
    Christian fundamentalist beliefs about,
        65–6
adversative training, 129–31
Aetna Insurance Company, 11
African Americans, 20, 46, 120
    as live-in help in white homes, 13
    participatory democracy and, 181,
        184–5
    voting by, 160–2
after-school programs, 36, 39–40, 57
agrarian economy, 81
AIDS, 71, 73, 95
Air Force, U.S., 75–6, 133
Alexander, Lamar, 177
Alliance for the Mentally Ill, 36
American Broadcasting Company (ABC),
    93
American Political Science Association,
    Status of Women Committee of, 151
American Renewal, 108
American Spectator, The, 104
Archer, Bill, 116
Arkansas, 77, 172
    Department of Health, 67, 69, 70

Army, U.S., 131–3
Asians, 20
Aspin, Les, 125, 126
attorney general, female nominees for,
    3–25, 102
au pairs, 31–2, 57

Bailyn, Lotte, 52–4, 153–4
Baird, Zoë, 5, 8, 11–16, 19–23, 25, 31, 67,
    76, 102, 125, 160, 161, 163
Baker, Nancy Kassebaum, 132
Balanced Budget Act (1997), 37
Balin, Jane, 196n7
Bane, Mary Jo, 3–5, 7–8, 29
Barber, Benjamin, 180
Bible, 65–6
Biden, Joseph, 8, 12–16, 20
Bill of Rights, 26
blacks, *see* African Americans
Blair, Anita, 140, 144
Blair, Tony, 135
Boorda, Adm. Jeremy, 126–8, 195n7
Bork, Robert, 143
Born, Brooksley, 18
Bosnia, 5, 134

Boston Globe, 40, 165
Boy Scouts of America, 72
Brady, Henry E., 179
Brazelton, T. Berry, 111
breast cancer, 19, 47
Breyer, Stephen, 26, 130
Bright Horizons, Inc., 33
Britain, 135, 153
Broder, David S., 28
Browning, Frank, 95
Buchanan, Constance, 106–7
Bush, George, 27, 123, 125, 133, 172

cabinet appointments, female, 3–25
Call to Renewal, 46–7
campaign financing, 177–8
Caring for Justice (West), 111
Carroll, James, 169
Carter, Jimmy, 5, 121, 122
Carville, James, 46
Catholics, 20, 46, 93, 108, 109–10
Center for Military Readiness, 132
Chasin, Laura, 185
child care, 31–6, 57–8, 115–16
    by au pairs, 31–2
    in day-care centers, 32–5
    and equality in workplace, 144
    by illegal-immigrant nannies, 11–15,
        20
    inadequate, crime and, 24
    as low-wage work for women, 21
    in private homes, 35
    by relatives, 35–6
    training for providers of, 57
    welfare reform and need for, 42, 141
Children's Defense Fund, 4, 103
Christian Coalition, 70, 91, 108
Christianity
    during Reformation, 106
    fundamentalist, 65, 72, 79, 89, 93, 108
        (*see also* Christian Coalition)
Citadel, The, 129, 131, 195*n*8
citizenship, corporate, 55
Citizens United, 172
Civil Rights Act (1964), 144
civil rights movement, 179

Clinton, Bill, 3–8, 17–18, 24, 45, 177,
    194*n*16
    attorney general nominees of, 8, 12–16,
        19, 20, 22, 23, 25
    day-care initiative of, 58, 116, 136
    Elders and, 66–7, 69, 70, 73
    Guinier and, 160–4
    family focus of 1996 campaign of,
        46–8, 55, 135
    health care plan of, 28–9, 115, 172
    home care tax credit proposed by, 56
    impeachment of, 78, 164
    leadership mode of, 165–70
    sexual indiscretions of, 3, 77, 105,
        135–6, 170–1, 173–4
    Supreme Court appointments of, 26,
        128, 130
    town meetings of, 174–5
    warrior-citizen tradition challenged by,
        123–8, 134–5
    and welfare reform, 29
    and Whitewater investigation, 172–3
Clinton, Hillary Rodham, 4, 5, 17, 103–6,
    114, 134, 160, 171, 177, 194*n*16
    and day-care initiative, 116
    health care plan of, 103, 104, 115, 172
    and Lewinsky affair, 78, 105
    and Whitewater investigation, 173
Cohen, William, 76, 133
combat, women in, 126, 127
communicative democracy, *see* participa-
    tory democracy
Communism, 121, 122
communitarians, 90–1, 150
community-based care, 36
Concerned Women for America, 108
condoms, 68, 70–4, 172
Congress, U.S., 15, 72, 73, 107, 116, 140, 171
    health care plan defeated in, 103
    and Lewinsky affair, 77, 105, 169
    Republican control of, 5, 29, 136, 172–3
    women in, 17, 18
    and women in military, 126, 128, 132
Constitution, U.S., 26, 128, 155
    Fourteenth Amendment, 125, 129
Contract with America, 72
Converse College, South Carolina Institute
    of Leadership for Women at, 129

Corning Corporation, 53
Corporate Citizenship Conference, 55
Corporate Family Solutions, Inc., 33
corporate-financed day care, 33–4, 52, 54
covenant marriage, 91
Craig, Larry, 116
Crittenden, Danielle, 141
Cultural Contradictions of Motherhood, The
    (Hays), 112
cumulative voting, 161

Dalton, John H., 195*n*7
day care, 32–5, 57, 116
    corporate-financed, 33–4, 52, 54
Defense Department, U.S., 126
deinstitutionalization, 36
deliberative democracy, *see* participatory
    democracy
Democratic Party, 5, 13, 47, 71–3, 103, 122
    Leadership Council, 46
Depression, the, 30, 121
DeVault, Marjorie, 49–50
Dionne, E. J., Jr., 46
disabled
    home health care for, 36–9, 58
    special education programs for, 39
divorce, 64, 75, 82, 84, 90–2
Dodson, Lisa, 35, 142, 180
Dole, Robert, 47, 124, 134–5
domestic violence, 19, 83
domestic work, contribution to national
    wealth of, 51
Donnelly, Elaine, 132
Don't Call Us Out of Name (Dodson), 180
double standard, sexual, 76, 78
drugs, legalization of, 71
Dubious Conceptions (Luker), 74–5
due process, 26
Duffey, Joseph, 32
Dukakis, Michael, 123

economic change, 81
Economic Policy Institute, 46
Edelman, Marian Wright, 4

Edelman, Peter, 3–5, 29
Edsall, Thomas Byrne, 46
Eisenhower, Dwight D., 122
elderly, home care for, 12–13, 25, 36–9,
    58–9
Elders, Joycelyn, 5, 8, 67–73, 82, 86, 87,
    125, 160, 173
Ellwood, David, 8
empathy, 168–9
Enlightenment, the, 170
Episcopal church, 93
equal opportunity, 16–17, 138–55
    antidiscrimination law and, 144
    care issues in, 150, 152–5
    conservative positions on, 140–3, 150
    feminist positions on, 150–2
    leadership and, 164
    sexual harassment and, 145–9
Equal Opportunity Employment Commis-
    sion, 145
Ettelbrick, Paula, 94–5
Etzioni, Amitai, 91
Ewing Marion Kauffman Foundation,
    190*n*7
Eyer, Diane, 111

Families and Work Institute, 34, 35, 59,
    189*n*5
family day care, 35, 57
Family and Medical Leave Act (1993), 25,
    27–8, 47, 55
Family Research Council, 108
Faux, Jeff, 46
feminists, antifamily charges against,
    150–2
Ferraro, Geraldine, 105
Fine, Michelle, 196*n*7
Fineman, Martha, 117
Fishkin, James, 182
Fleet Financial Services, 54
Fletcher, Joyce, 154
flextime, 52, 53
Flinn, Lt. Kelly, 75–6
Focus on the Family, 108
Folbre, Nancy, 51
food, sharing of, 49

Foote, Evelyn, 132
Foster, Vincent, 177
free-market rhetoric, *see* private, ideology
　of
Frum, David, 93, 95

gay men and lesbians, 46, 64, 78–9, 110
　attitude of conservatives toward, 65, 66,
　　73
　discrimination against, 72
　family law issues for, 84
　marriage of, 92–6
　in military, 5, 172
Georgetown University, 4, 168
Germany, 153
Ginsburg, Ruth Bader, 125, 128–31
Girl Scouts of America, 72
Great Society, 139, 171, 183
Greece, ancient, 120, 121
Greenberg, Stanley, 46
Greider, William, 177
Grenada, U.S. invasion of, 122
group identification, 20
guaranteed annual income, 57
Guinier, Lani, 4, 5, 20, 160–4, 177,
　196n7
Gulf War, 123

Habermas, Jürgen, 197n6
Haiti, U.S. intervention in, 5, 134
Harman, Jane, 135
Harper's Magazine, 140
Harvard University, 8, 162, 183
　Kennedy School of Government, 4
　Leadership Education Project, 166
Hays, Sharon, 112, 113
Head Start, 183–4
Healey, Ronald, 55
health care, 5, 28–9
　Clinton plan for, 103, 104, 115, 172
　for elderly and disabled, 36–9
　public-school based, 40, 68–70
　30/40 plan in, 55
　universal, 58, 71
　women and, 19

Heifetz, Ronald, 166
Hewlett, Sylvia Ann, 150, 153
Hill, Anita, 12, 125, 145, 163
Hispanics, 21
Hochschild, Arlie, 53
home health care, 25, 37–9, 58
　by illegal immigrants, 12–13, 39
homosexuals, *see* gay men and lesbians
House of Representatives, U.S., 5, 72,
　126
　Armed Services Committee, 125
　Ways and Means Committee, 116
housing allowances, 58
Humphrey, Hubert, 122
Hussein, Saddam, 123

illegal immigrants
　child care by, 5, 11–15, 21, 102
　home health care by, 25, 39
inclusion, politics of, 161–2, 167–9,
　176–87
income supports, 57
Independent Women's Forum (IWF), 140,
　141, 146
Individual Education Plans, 39
industrialization, 51, 81
intimate relations, familial, 83–5
Iran hostage crisis, 122
Iran-contra affair, 172
It Takes a Village (Hillary Clinton), 104

Japan, 153
Japanese Americans, 120
Jefferson Center for New Democratic
　Processes, 181
Jews, 20, 110
John Paul II, Pope, 109
Johnson, Haynes, 28
Johnson, Lyndon, 7, 122, 139
Joint Chiefs of Staff, 76
Jones, Kathleen, 185–6
Jones, Paula, 77, 146–7, 174
Justice Department, U.S., 11, 19
　Civil Rights Division, 4
Justice, Gender, and the Family (Okin), 59

Kaminer, Wendy, 140
Kelly, Michael, 165
Kelson, Adm. Frank, 126
Kennedy, Edward, 32, 71
Kennedy, John F., 122
Kerry, John, 32
Knowledge University, 33
Kurz, Demie, 92

labor movement, 19, 154
LaHaye, Beverly, 108
Lakeoff, Robin, 123
Larson, Adm. Charles, 127
Lawrence, Joan, 41–2
Leach, Penelope, 111
leadership
    adversarial training for, 129–31
    demasculinized, 135–6
    democratically inclusive mode of,
        164–75
Legal Services Corporation, 103, 171
Leonard, Mary, 105
Lerner, Michael, 194*n*16
lesbians, *see* gay men and lesbians
Lewinsky, Monica, 77, 105, 135–6, 147,
    148, 165, 169
Lincoln, Abraham, 120
listening ability, 167–8
lobbying, 178, 179
long-term care, 36–9, 58–9
Louisiana, marriage contract in, 91
low-wage workers, 21
    in child-care centers, 34
    in home care for elderly and disabled, 38
    subsidies for, 57
Ludtke, Melissa, 88–9
Luker, Kristin, 74

Magaziner, Ira, 103
Marine Corps, U.S., 127, 133
Marine Hospital Service, 67
Mariner, Capt. Rosemary, 132–3
Marshner, Connie, 108
Mary Baldwin College, Virginia Women's
    Institute for Leadership at, 129

masculine authority, primacy of,
    see warrior-citizen tradition
Massachusetts
    Commission on Father Absence and
        Family Support, 87
    Senate Ways and Means Committee, 181
    Small Necessities Leave Act, 55–6
    Supreme Judicial Court, 51–4, 153
Massachusetts Institute of Technology
    (MIT), 162
    Sloan School of Management, 52
masturbation, 73
Medicaid, 37, 58, 71
Medicare, 37, 38, 47, 58
mental illness, 36–7, 58
Meritor Savings Bank v. Vinson (1986), 145
merit principle, 18–19, 21, 102
military
    gay men in, 5, 172
    women in, 125–33, 148
Milken, Michael, 33
Miramax Films, 93
Mitsubishi Motors of America, 149
Morris, Dick, 46, 47, 135
Motherguilt (Eyer), 111
motherhood, 101–18
    contradictory ideologies of, 111–12
    and ethic of care, 113–14
    religious concepts of, 106–10, 113
    unwed, 74–5, 86–9
    work and, *see* child care
MTV, 134
Mulieris Dignitatem (John Paul II), 109
Murphy Brown (television show), 88
Muschamp, Herbert, 166
Muskie, Edmund, 122
Muslim fundamentalism, 122

nannies, 31
    illegal immigrant, 5, 11–15, 20, 21, 102
National Assessment of Educational
    Progress (NAEP), 190*n*11
National Conference of Catholic Bishops,
    110
National Institute of Mental Health, 36
National Issues Convention, 182, 198*n*11
Navy, U.S., 125–8, 132, 133

New Deal, 5, 7, 29, 115
New Labour Party, British, 135
New Left, 171
Newsweek, 128
New York State, family day care regulation in, 35
New York Times, The, 5, 72, 127–8, 162
    Magazine, 114
Nicaragua, 122, 172
Nixon, Richard, 122, 171
nuclear arms race, 122
nursing homes, 25, 38, 39

Ohio, welfare reform in, 41–2
Okin, Susan Moller, 59
Oklahoma City bombing, 168, 177
opinion polling, 178
    deliberative, 182
out-of-wedlock births, 74–5, 86–9

Packwood, Bob, 145, 147
paid leaves, 56
participatory democracy, 180–87
part-time work, 52, 53
Paul VI, Pope, 109
Perot, Ross, 177
Personal Responsibility and Work Opportunity Act, 50
petitioning, 178, 179
Pew Charitable Trust, 190*n*7
Pew Research Center for the People and the Press, 113
Phelps, Edmund, 57, 88, 153
Philander Smith College, 68
Planned Parenthood, 114
Portzamparc, Christian de, 166
poverty, 140, 180
    and blockages to opportunity, 139, 142
    and out-of-wedlock births, 74, 87
    pathologies produced by, 57
    public health issues of, 67–8
    and socially supported care, 50
Powers, Katherine, 179–80

pregnancy
    and equality in workplace, 144
    teenage, 40, 64, 68, 70–2, 74, 87
Presidential Libraries, 182
privacy, familial, 82–3
private, ideology of, 26–7, 44, 177
    authority in, 121, 138–55
    child care and, 42
    health care and, 28–9
Promise Keepers, 89
proportional representation (PR), 161, 162
Protestants, 46, 106, 110
    right-wing, 108–9
    see also specific denominations
protest movements, 178–9
    antiwar, 123, 171
Public Broadcasting Company, 182
Public Conversations Project, 185, 198*n*11
Public Health Service, 67

Quayle, Dan, 88
Quayle, Marilyn, 104
quotas, 5, 162

Radcliffe Public Policy Institute, 151
Ralston, Gen. Joseph W., 76
rape, 19
Rayner, Richard, 131
Reagan, Ronald, 4, 122–3, 127, 172
Redemptoris Mater (John Paul II), 109
redistricting, 161–3
referenda, 177
Reformation, 106
Reno, Janet, 23
reproductive technologies, 84
Republican Party, 5, 29, 57, 72, 78, 104, 116, 136, 172, 173, 177
    Senate Policy Committee, 116
Riley, Richard, 165–6
Robert's Rules of Order, 183, 184
Rubenstein, Carin, 59
Rutherford Institute, 173

same-sex marriage, 92–6
Scholzman, Kay Lehman, 179
schools, services provided by, 39–41
  health care, 40, 68, 69
Schroeder, Patricia, 27, 125, 126
Schultz, Vicki, 148–9, 196*n*8
Schwarz, John, 57, 88
Senate, U.S., 5, 15, 72, 78, 126, 162, 163,
    169, 173
  Judiciary Committee, 8, 11, 12, 14, 145,
    162–3
  Labor and Human Resources Commit-
    tee, 70–1
  Republican Policy Committee, 116
"separate but equal," 129
sex education, 40, 68–71, 73
sexual harassment, 145–9
  in military, 125, 131–3
sexual morality, 63–79, 81, 82, 173
  adultery and, 75–8
  Christian fundamentalist views of, 65–
    66
  divorce and, 90
  Elders's policies and, 67–73
  gay marriage and, 92
  unmarried mothers and, 74–5, 88
Shalala, Donna, 71
Shanley, Mary Lyndon, 84
single parents, 64, 66, 84, 86–9
Skocpol, Theda, 96
Skolnick, Arlene, 45, 91
Slouching Towards Gomorrah (Bork), 143
sociability work, 49–50
social morality, 80–97
  of care and equality, 85
  divorce and, 90–2
  of intimate relations, 83–5
  leadership and, 164
  motherhood and, 114–15
  out-of-wedlock births and, 86–9
  of privacy, 82–3
  same-sex marriage and, 92–6
Social Security, 36, 56, 141
Social Security Domestic Employment
    Reform Act (1994), 15–16
Social Security taxes, 11, 12, 14
Somalia, U.S. intervention in, 5, 133–4
Southern Baptist Convention, 93, 108

Soviet Union, 122
special education programs, 40
Special Prosecutor's Office, 171–4
Spock, Benjamin, 111
Stacey, Judith, 91
Starr, Kenneth, 77, 172–3
Stearns, Cliff, 72
Stevenson, Adlai, 122
Sullivan, Andrew, 95
supermajority mechanism, 161–2
Supreme Court, U.S., 26, 125, 128–30, 145,
    148, 149, 195*n*8
Sweden, paid leave in, 56
Switzerland, paid leave in, 56
System, The (Johnson and Broder), 28

Tailhook scandal, 125, 127
Tandem Computers, 53
tax credits, 56–7
  for day care, 57, 116
teenagers, 49
  pregnancy-prevention programs for, 87
  sexually active, 40, 64, 68, 70–2, 74
Texas, University of, 182
30/40 plan, 55
Thomas, Clarence, 12, 125, 145
town meetings, 174–5
Tragedies of Our Own Making (Neely), 40
Tronto, Joan, 49
True Womanhood, cult of, 107

U.S. News and World Report, 55
United Church of Christ, 93
United Nations, 5, 73, 173
United States Information Agency (USAI),
    31, 33
unwed mothers, *see* out-of-wedlock births
Upton v. JWP Businessland (1997), 51–3, 153,
    191*n*11

Verba, Sidney, 179
Vietnam War, 122, 127, 128, 195*n*7
  protests against, 123, 171

violence against women, 19, 83
  legislation on, 47
Virginia Military Institute (VMI), 125,
  128–31, 195*n*8
Visiting Nurses Association, 38
voting, 176
  lowering of age for, 121
  by minorities, 160–2, 178
Voting Rights Act (1965), 160

Wall Street Journal, The, 116, 162
Walt Disney Corporation, 93
War on Poverty, 115
warrior-citizen tradition, 119–37, 171–2,
  174
  Clinton's departure from, 123–7, 134–6,
    165, 168, 171, 172
  history of, 120–2
  and women in military, 125–33
Watergate scandal, 122
Wattenberg, Daniel, 104
Webb, James, 127–8
Weldon, Fay, 135
welfare reform, 3–5, 8, 29–30, 50, 136,
  141, 173

child care needs and, 35, 42, 56–7
out-of-wedlock births and, 74, 86
responsibility and, 89
West, Cornel, 150, 153
West, Robin, 111, 113
Wever, Kirsten, 56
White, Edmund, 95
White, Lucie, 183–4
Whitewater scandal, 172–3
Wolfe, Alan, 193*n*15
Women Strike for Peace, 107
Women's Ordination Conference, 110
Wood, Kimba, 14–15, 25
Woodward, Louise, 32
workplace
  equal opportunity in, 138–55
  family care policy in, 51–7
World AIDS Day, 73
World War II, 134

Xerox Corporation, 53

Zumwalt, Adm. Elmo R., Jr., 195*n*7